Memoir:
I Came. I Saw. I Stayed.

by

ALMA D. READY

foreword by Axel C. Holm

afterword by Patrick D. Simpson, editor

A woman's life-long search for a home through four unhappy marriages – and the amazing things she did when she found one in Nogales, Arizona, a busy border-crossing town with a society all its own. As a stranger in this strange land, Alma Ready's path was a rocky one, but ultimately one that led to her career as a well-known Arizona writer, photographer, journalist and historian.

"I have been very happy here. The country is beautiful, the 'Border Culture' fascinating, the people friendly and the climate near-perfect. This is where I feel at home."

– Alma D. Ready

DEDICATION

On the occasion of the 100th Anniversary of the 1914 City Hall in Nogales, Arizona (February 15, 2015), I dedicate this book to my mother, Alma D. Ready, who was instrumental in establishing the Pimeria Alta Museum there—and whom I loved and regarded as the most unforgettable person in my life, and from whose genes and inspiration I inherited a love for travel, photography and a burning desire to write about history.

I have also digitized Mom's four books and made them available at **www.booksbypatricksimpson.com**. 100% of her Kindle book royalties will be donated to the Pimeria Alta Historical Society and Museum.

Open Range and Hidden Silver
Calabasas
Nogales, Arizona 1880-1980 Centennial Anniversary
A Very Small Place

— Patrick Simpson, editor

CONTENTS

ACKNOWLEDGMENTS

My profound thanks to Axel C.F. Holm, Teresa Leal, the people of Nogales in both Arizona and Mexico, and to those who not only brought the Pimeria Alta Historical Society into being in 1948 and dedicated the Museum in Old City Hall in 1980, but to those who have kept them running since. Most of all, I dedicate this book to the Lord Jesus Christ for His glory and honor.

FOREWORD

by Axel C.F. Holm

Few can describe their lives much less write it as if a suspenseful novel yet with blunt, self effacing honesty. Alma Ready's *Memoir* is not a tell all, but she tells all, the unpretentious story of her life growing up in World War I, becoming a young woman in the raucous, roaring twenties, surviving the Great Depression, her four marriages of convenience and romance, producing four children and wrenchingly forced to surrender three, and growing up again in World War II to find her true calling as a photographer, historian and author.

Photo courtesy of Axel C.F. Holm

I met Alma Ready in Tucson, Arizona in 1966 after meeting her youngest son, Johnny, as we trained together at Lowry Air Force Base, Colorado. An unassuming lady, Mrs. Ready took me aback with her great interest that I was from Nogales, Arizona and Santa Cruz County, that inconsequential little piece of the Gadsden Purchase of 1853 that forms the southwest border, now a vital place of national security. For me, it remains home and the place of my chosen career in my father's produce business. In 1966, I saw none of the magic, magnificence and majesty of my home later revealed through Alma Ready's eyes and words.

Soon after meeting Alma Ready, I was surprised to find that she, and her contemporary, my mother, Louise Holm, became friends. Both had ambitions to write, Alma about the story of Santa Cruz County and my mother about growing up in the Mexican Revolution. I paid little attention but if I happened upon one of their conversations, I observed each transfixed by the other with stories. 'Curious,' I underestimated. In due course, the first written history of Santa Cruz County, Alma Ready's *Open Range and Hidden Silver* became the talk and stuff of old timers. A few years later, Alma published her excellent bibliography entitled *A Very Small Place* and at great sacrifice, as she describes in the last pages of *Memoir*. Finally for the centennial of Nogales in 1980, Alma Ready wrote *The Nogales Centennial, 1880-1980*. Embittered by the lack of success of *A Very Small Place*, it nonetheless became the guide and road map for future historians eager to find the hidden gold that is the history of Santa Cruz County. I know, because I became one of those future historians following Alma's blazed trail to persuade the county Board of Supervisors to add to Santa Cruz County, a tag line, 'Birthplace of Arizona History'.

Well after the death of my mother and then of Alma Ready, I grew up enough to respect the past and to become involved in the Pimeria Alta Historical Society, and like Alma, found myself transfixed by the story of the ground on which I was born. As president of the Pimeria Alta Historical Society, I discovered just how much work Alma did to put the basics of the story of places, people and events that coalesced in this small piece of the Gadsden Purchase. Along with her chronicles, Alma left a collection of thousands of photographs, each of which is worth a thousand words, produced through her keen and creative vision.

Alma Ready's discovery and honest interpretation of our local history is revealed in her story, *Memoir*, indeed a mirror of much of the American story in the twentieth century, to find economic stability and peaceful purpose impeded by cataclysms and constrictions and entangling relationships. Alma Ready matured and found her way, while our nation continues its' struggles. *Memoir* is her account of the people, places and events in her life and her coming of age as a photographer, historian and author. Alma Ready's story is the story of the 20th century.

— Axel C. F. Holm

***

Noted Nogales native and historian Axel C.F. Holm has served on the Arizona Historical Society State Board and chaired the state Library, Archive and Collections Committee. Having written more than fifty local history articles, including many for the local Eco magazine, he is motivated to keep a record of the history of Nogales as well as promoting the importance of the border cities which he would like to see as a "think tank" for Latin American studies. More recently, Axel served as Grand Marshall for Nogales's 2012 annual Christmas Light Parade, with a theme of "Christmas Then and Now" in honor of Arizona's centennial celebration.

Axel has written about Alma Ready before: a nearly 4-page article dubbed "Alma Ready, Nogales' Hidden Treasure" in the October-November 2008 issue of *Pimeria Post*, a newsletter of the Pimeria Alta Museum and Historical Society. As past president of the society, Axel wrote: "Alma Ready came to the southwest from the east sixty-six years ago and discovered a land of enchantment. No person before or since has found the magic of our history and worked so hard to save it, document it and show it. Alma gave new life to the Pimeria Alta Historical Society."

— Patrick Simpson

***

INTRODUCTION

Dear Reader,

My Mom died on May 29, 2003 at the age of ninety-five. Among her belongings was *Memoir*, an unpublished manuscript she'd written some ten years earlier. I soon found myself immersed in this compelling "tell all" about her life. It was as if this beautiful, very-talented only child from south New Jersey had wanted each of her four children, three of whom she'd barely known, and anyone else who'd known her, to know the full story of her lifelong journey to the Arizona border town of Nogales. It was in Nogales that she finally took root as a locally famous photographer, writer, and as a driving force behind the Pimeria Alta Historical Museum.

Memoir is a confession, if you will, with perhaps the hope that people would walk in her shoes for awhile, and then somehow understand her – and perhaps even forgive her.

So why have I waited so long to publish it myself? I can't say why… I just know that I have to – and I have to do it now. If I don't, who will? In the words of Christ, "Honor your father and mother…" (Matthew 19:19, NIV).

Other than a couple of minor proofreading changes, I didn't add, delete or change anything in *Memoir*. I did, however, add many notes, such as "ARJ" (Alma Ready's Journal) or "pds" (my initials) indicated in brackets [ ]. I also added a foreword by Axel Holm, an afterword, and many graphics and photos – mainly from Mom's photo albums and my own.

I am Mom's first son from her third marriage and the first to tell her story. She is – and always will be – the most fascinating person I've ever met. Others have hated her, others have loved her, but no one could ever forget her. Count me as one who loved her, and always will.

But judge for yourself, dear Reader. Read on…

— Patrick Simpson

1 – PORT NORRIS, NEW JERSEY

[pds: Port Norris, New Jersey – a small town located where the Maurice River meets the Delaware Bay. Established in 1811, the town has a rich history as a major center for oysters. Less than an hour's drive NW from Cape May where, during the 19th century, the rich and famous traveled by steamboat and railroad from Philadelphia, Baltimore, and Washington D.C. Notables included Presidents James Buchanan, Franklin Pierce and Ulysses S. Grant.]

2014 view of Old Firehouse - 1741 Main Street, Port Norris, New Jersey

My mother's parents [pds: **Edgar and Sallie B. Henderson (nee Shropshire)**] shared their house with a fire engine. I don't know where the horses lived but I remember occasionally hearing the team clop-clop over the planks of the bridge which crossed the ditch next door then a quick succession of subdued noises followed by the rumble of iron-bound wheels as the whole assembly emerged from the other side of the house and dashed clangorously down the street. Whether half of a two-family house was converted to accommodate the fire company or it was originally built that way I never knew. And now there is no one left who remembers.

Until I was six my mother [pds: **Ada Henderson Duffield**] and I used to visit there often. We lived in Cedarville where my father [pds: **Philip S. Duffield**] was station agent for the New Jersey Southern Railroad.

1

[ARJ]: "My Grandfather, Edgar Henderson, was tall and handsome with 'salt-and-pepper' thick, wavy hair, as I remember him. He built oyster boats 'down at the cove' (the Maurice River Cove on the Delaware Bay) a few minutes' trolley ride from Port Norris where they lived.

"Grandma's maiden name was Sallie (Sarah) Heisler and she was from Heislerville, five or six miles down on the cove. I remember going there once. My mother was a great visitor and she used to drag me around, to various aunts, all of whom seemed to me to be on their last legs. Grandma and Grandpa Henderson had five children: My mother, Ada; Uncle Clarence; Aunt Alma: Uncle Howard; and Uncle Amos.

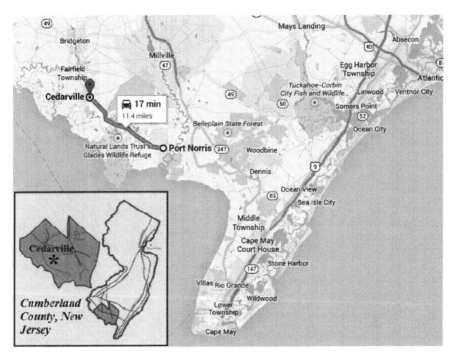

"Port Norris was at the end of both the railroad and the trolley line from Bridgeton, through Cedarville. It was in a swamp and the town was crisscrossed with drainage ditches crossed by rumbling wooden bridges. Water snakes cruised the ditches and mosquitoes were fierce. My mother and I visited there often, going down on the trolley, and one time Daddy sent me down on the train in the caboose. Distance twelve miles.

"The station was from where farmers from the surrounding area shipped produce to Philadelphia and New York. They also brought great wagonloads to the two or three canning factories, especially pumpkins and tomatoes. Daddy was still living at home and supporting his parents when at age 35 he met my mother. "]

It was only half an hour's ride on the trolley down to "the Port" (Port Norris, center of the lower Delaware Bay oyster industry). I think mother probably was a little homesick, especially for her lively younger sister [pds: **Alma Shropshire Henderson**]. Daddy was 15 years older and. a little stodgy.

[pds: From the *Arizona Republic*, March 1985: "Since the days of the Colonies, the waters of Delaware Bay off Port Norris have yielded some of the finest-tasting oysters in the country. Port Norris is where the Maurice River joins Delaware Bay. It's the spot from which about 95 percent of all oysters in the state are harvested. It is a gray, weather-worn area that wears oyster shells the way a woman wears pearls, a place that old-timers refer to as Shelltown."]

There is a series of very clear pictures of the Port in my mind. A water snake unconcernedly drifting with the current down the ditch which bordered the back lawn. (The town was built on a partially reclaimed swamp; clouds of mosquitoes were a matter of course as were the daily chores of trimming the lamp wicks and fetching drinking water from one of the "good" wells across the street.) Playing house with a neighbor's daughter in the

Electric trolley, owned by the Bridgeton and Millville Traction Company, serving Cedarville & Port Norris from 1893-1922.

spreading limbs of a huge willow growing in the swamp behind her house. The damp-smelling woodshed at the bottom of Grandma's lot where the fat snails that lived among the stacks of old newspapers would curl up and die if you sprinkled them with salt. The ill-lighted little store up the street where the grocer kept two guinea pigs in little cages. Straight-faced, he told me that if you picked them up by the tail their eyes would fall out, and I believed it for years.

You entered Grandma's house through the living room directly from the little stoop. Sliding doors sealed off the parlor where the piano lived. Dominating the living room was the big roll-top desk under which I was allowed to play house, and opposite the entrance was the door to the dark, steep stairway to the second floor. Most "living", however, was done in the dining room where, in addition to the big cloth covered table, there was a comfortable couch and a cupboard where my toys were kept. Sprawled on the floor there, I spent hours playing jackstraws or tiddlywinks or listening to Grandpa reading the Sunday comics which he saved up for me. Mutt and Jeff and the Katzenjammer Kids.

Alma's family, Thanksgiving 1912. (top left): Uncle Clarence Henderson, Grandpa Edgar Henderson, Philip S. Duffield (Dad), Uncle Howard Henderson. (bottom left): Grandma "Sallie" (Shropshire) Henderson, Aunt Mable (Clarence's wife), Aunt Alma Henderson, Alma H. Duffield, Mary "Auntie Mame" (Howard's wife).

If we went to the Port on a weekday, we usually missed my grandfather. Along with most of the men in town, he took the early trolley "down to the landing" where he worked as a ship's carpenter, building oyster boats. When the four-o'clock south-bound trolley made the turn toward the landing – right in front of Grandma's next-door neighbor's – Mother and I had just time enough to put on our coats and get our things together before the trolley was back, had racketed up to the end of the street, had its pole reversed and returned to where we were waiting in front of the house.

Upstairs, if we stayed all night, I slept between Mother and her sister in the big wide bed with the carved walnut headboard. The marble-topped wash stand held a bowl and pitcher and tooth mug. On the bureau were the "ivory" (celluloid) toilet set, including a hair receiver, a hairpin tray and a button hook. Also a round, cardboard box of face powder with a small chamois. The chamber pot was genteelly hidden within a commode. When I was put down for a nap on a sultry summer afternoon, I could hear the cheerful ringing of the anvil in the blacksmith's shop just across the ditch.

My favorite room was the parlor, and until later when I learned to play the piano, my favorite place in the parlor was the big bay window. The whole bay was hung with vertically hinged wooden shutters fitted with tiny adjustable louvers. I was fascinated by the louvers. Section by section, I would close them to subdue the light, then starting at the beginning again, open them to admit the afternoon sun.

Aunt Alma was not a sit-by-the-fireside spinster, however. In her early twenties, she was warm and loving and had a kind of effervescence. She liked to dance and sing and in her music cabinet, along with "Aura Lee" and "I Love You Truly" and other such sheet music were pieces like "Take Me Out to the Ball Park", and "Everybody's Doing What, the Turkey Trot." Her friends were a fun-loving crowd. Often they would gather round the piano and spend the whole evening singing and drinking lemonade or root beer. On holidays the whole family congregated and there was music of two coronets, a harmonica, a "sweet potato" and an accordion.

Then she met Sam [pds: Veltman]. A neighbor and long-time friend had just returned from a vacation in North Jersey and brought Sam home with him for a visit. He probably came partly because he was curious about life in the boondocks, but he had a beautiful voice and fit right in. There appeared to be an irresistible attraction between Alma and Sam. In two weeks they were married and he had whisked her away to another part of the country and a new way of life. Less than a year later she came back to Port Norris to await the birth of their child. They exchanged letters for several weeks and then he stopped writing. She never saw him again. By the time I visited the Port again, the baby was nine months old and Alma had picked up where she left off at the Wessels.

[ARJ: "Alma and Sam had lived at Lake Hopatcong in northern New Jersey, a fashionable summer resort where Sam owned a lot of property (boat concessions, etc.). A friend of the family later looked for him there only to discover that he'd sold all his property and disappeared. When Dotty was in college a lawyer wrote to her mother and said Sam had died and they were looking for his heirs. Seems he left quite a bundle and it all went to Dotty. Aunt Alma got nothing. After Grandma died she kept house for Uncle Howard until he died. Then she moved into an apartment and later followed Dotty to Phoenix."]

Aunt Alma's red-headed baby, Dorothy.

2 – Cedarville, New Jersey

[ARJ: "My father's parents, Albert and Louisa (Shaw) Duffield, lived in a small frame house on a road along the railroad tracks about a mile from downtown Cedarville. They had three boys: Nelson ("Bob"), Philip and Elmer. Grandma died when 1 was about four years old and Grandpa went to live with Uncle Nelson and Aunt Georgie. Uncle Elmer moved into the old house which was next door. Both places had about an acre which they put into  vegetables. Grandpa was all bent over, had a high little voice and a long white beard and sat in a chair on the porch all day with his hands resting on a cane. I don't remember ever talking to him."]

Cedarville, 1915. Alma, with 1st cousins Elmer, Jr. (l.) and Warren Duffield.

[ARJ: "Daddy's other brother, Elmer, married a widow with one child, Lillian, ten years older than I. I kept in touch with her through high school but not after that, My Aunt Jennie was plump and jolly and raised violets in a cold frame. Uncle Elmer read meters for the gas company. They had two boys, Warren, my age, and Elmer Jr., two years younger. We used to play together once in a while."]

My mother and father and I had moved to Virginia and back to New Jersey again, but not to our old home. This peripatetic pattern was to govern our lives as long as Mother was alive. Always we moved to a new home and settled in "for good" only to have fate decree otherwise.

I was only seven when we left Cedarville but there are certain scenes and events which I remember as though it were yesterday. One was my father's office at the railroad station where he took me sometimes on Sunday when he had work to catch up.

I liked to listen to the strange rhythm of the telegraph key. I liked to watch as Daddy took letter-size sheets of sturdy cloth from a pail of water, ran them through a hand-operated wringer and placed them neatly between sheets of thin, tough paper atop a report or letter written in purplish indelible ink, the whole sandwich built on a metal platform beneath the wheel of a heavy cast-iron device called a letter press. Using both hands and considerable muscle, he then turned the wheel, forcing the upper plate down to squeeze the daylights out of the sandwich. What emerged were several damp and slightly smudged copies of the original, to be spread out to dry then mailed out or placed between the heavy covers of a file book.

The job done, we would walk half a mile down the track, turn off into the piney woods and emerge at the edge of Uncle Nelson's chicken farm. Aunt Georgie usually would be down in the basement sorting eggs and wiping with a damp cloth any egg accidentally besmirched by a careless hen.

While Daddy and his brother inspected the poultry runs, I was allowed to ride the foot-propelled grindstone pretending I was traveling off to some faraway place. Like Uncle Nelson.

During the gold rush to the Klondike in 1898, while Daddy stayed home and took care of their fragile old folks, Nelson, known as "Bob" in Dawson City, struck it rich. At least rich enough to buy a chicken farm in Oregon and when that didn't pan out, to come back and start over just a few miles from the family home. He brought a wife with him, a woman we found rather

strange

, Georgie wore overalls for one thing, cut her grizzled curly hair close to the scalp, and worked on the farm like a man. Looking back, I suspect that she had put up part of the money for the venture. I also suspect that she might

Miners and packers climbing the Chilkoot Pass, September 1898, during the Klondike Gold Rush. Nelson still lived in Alaska's Birch Creek area in 1900. He married Georgie "Bessie" in 1902.

have earned her share as a dance hall hostess. She had a trunk full of clothes like I had never seen — nor did I ever see her wear them — shiny silks and satins in scarlet and green and purple, with lots of sparkly beads. Originally from England, she had arrived in the Klondike via the gold fields of South Africa with a husband who had not survived. She and Uncle Nelson lived quietly. In the evening they listened to their Victrola with the cylindrical records or played cribbage, keeping score on a pegboard made of a heavy, hand-carved walrus tusk. They had one of the first automobiles in the area, a big five-passenger touring car, but it was used only on business trips to the county seat.

Robert Nelson Duffield (1924) with his dog Nort – and his 1923 Ford Model T Touring car.

I think my father would have liked to have a chicken farm too. Instead, he kept a few hens in a small house out of mother's sight at the foot of our lot and subscribed to a poultry magazine and *The Country Gentleman.* Daddy had a lot of self-control. I never heard him swear and he and Mother were confirmed teetotalers.

Mother read the *Ladies' Home Journal* and the latest novels. As befitting a former school teacher, she organized the first Parent-Teacher Association in town and taught me to read when I was five. She was an excellent cook but found no joy in housework. Which she did well, however, partly because she considered it her Duty and partly out of pride in her home.

[ARJ: "I think she was determined, above all things, to be a "lady" – and nearly killed herself and me trying to make one out of me. She succeeded pretty well with herself, however. I never heard anyone but her family call her by her first name. My Father called her "my lady" and everyone else, even members of her bridge club, called her Mrs. Duffield. Neither she nor my father were demonstrative. He literally adored her and spoiled her to the best of his ability, but he was older and serious-minded. She would have liked to dance and to travel, but they couldn't afford to travel and he wouldn't dance.

"Mother graduated from high school in 1902, took the teachers' exam (that's the way it was done in those days), taught three or four years, and married Daddy in 1906 at age twenty-one.

"When they were first married they lived in a rented house in Cedarville and had me. (She was injured in birthing me and not able to have more children.) Then they built their own house, very nice, good location."]

It was a home to be proud of, a handsome frame house on a quiet street shaded by old maples. The well-trimmed grassy lot sloped gently back to the vegetable garden then to the fringe of trees surrounding the mill pond. There was a wide verandah, a large living-room with an open stairway done in golden oak, a dining room and the family room where Mother placed her combination bookcase and desk and the upright piano Daddy had given her for a wedding present. Lamps were the latest, fueled by kerosene but with light-distributing mantles and sight-saving green glass shades. A hot-air furnace was installed in the basement.

Alma's home in Cedarville, New Jersey, 1913

In the kitchen were a golden oak kitchen cabinet, a modern four-burner kerosene range and a sink with a hand-pump and drain leading to a vigorous stand of canna lilies in the backyard. The kitchen also housed two of Mother's proudest possessions, a fireless cooker lined with red flannel, and a vacuum cleaner whose hose she manipulated while Daddy manned the hand pump.

Upstairs, in addition to three airy bedrooms there was a smaller, empty room labeled "bathroom" in anticipation of the time when the town might start construction of a municipal water system.

It wasn't our first home. We had lived in two rented houses previously, which I don't remember except the pile of oyster shells in the backyard on Main Street. As in most homes in town, when the season opened, the husband would stash a gunnysack of bivalves in the backyard and on many evenings could be seen shucking oysters just before supper. The shells were tossed in a pile which grew until the following spring pickup. My father followed the custom and at every third or fourth oyster, removed the "eye" and extended it to me on the tip of the oyster knife. I chewed and swallowed and waited open-mouthed for the next one. Oyster stew with Exton crackers usually followed, or sometimes oyster fritters.

No such shell pile disfigured the lawn at our new house. Daddy built a see-saw for me in the backyard and hung a sturdy swing from a limb of the big maple out front. He also let me play house between the rows of pole beans in the garden. Playing house always featured a bed for Nellie, my rag doll infant with the painted hair. Teddy bear was always dragged along too, even after I had squeezed all the stuffing out of the place where his elbow ought to be.

Cutting Ice on Cedarville Pond

Occasionally there were small excursions like a day on the beach at Fortescue on the Delaware Bay and being rowed out to the lighthouse where I was nearly scared out of my wits when someone accidentally rang the big bell under which I was standing. A day concluded by a shore dinner thoroughly enjoyed by the adults. I choked on a bone in my shad.

Daddy took me to the annual poultry show in Bridgeton one year. I enjoyed the trolley ride and looking at the funny-looking chickens, but the place did have a pungent odor and I could see why Mother preferred to stay home. And why she preferred to approach Daddy's chickens only after they had been beheaded, de-feathered and eviscerated.

The outing I shall always remember is gathering water lilies from a flat-bottomed boat in the shallows at the edge of the pond. I can feel the cool water up to my elbows, the long, thin, slippery stems in my fingers and the heaven-scented fresh breath of the blossoms as I buried my nose in their cool white faces.

Mother took me skating once or twice but I never learned to skate as well as she and her friends. I was more interested in watching the workmen over near the ice house, sawing big chunks out of the pond to be stored in sawdust for the coming summer. On winter Sundays I wore my little fur muff as we walked across the dam to church and Sunday school. Back home I could read or work in my coloring books. If Mother played the piano it was a hymn.

[ARJ: "My mother and father were very much involved with the church when I was a small child. They had both 'signed the pledge' – not a drop of liquor in the house – ever. Nor a Sunday paper. You played hymns only on the piano on Sunday."]

Things were different in Virginia.

3 – HOPEWELL, VIRGINIA

Daddy left first. Like many family men his age, he chose to serve his country during the Great War by working in a defense plant, the E.I. DuPont de Nemours ammunition factory at Hopewell, Virginia. Mother and I traveled by train to New York, by boat to Norfolk and up the James River to our new home.

[pds: Hopewell was developed by DuPont in 1914 as Hopewell Farm, an incorporated area in Prince George County. DuPont first built a dynamite factory there, then switched to the manufacture of guncotton during World War I. Alma's father served as supervisor of the guncotton line.]

(l): Our house in City Point, Va. (r): View of James River from DuPont.

Mother was transported. She seemed to view the whole affair as a great adventure. I simply accepted the situation, but I didn't understand. How could I? In our part of the world, children were not only "seen but not heard," they were not permitted to listen. Nothing more important than the weather was discussed in my presence. Not ever.

My World War I was an unexplained upheaval of our personal lives and in the sixth grade, a daily morning assembly where we belted out songs like "Over There" and "There's a Long, Long Trail A-Winding." I never saw a soldier.

Virginia, to me, was lazing away the summer in a lawn swing in the front lawn of a new bungalow, one of a row of attractive look-alikes just constructed for its supervisors by The Company.

[pds: The Company was in City Point, a town in Prince George County, Virginia located at the confluence of the Appomattox and James Rivers. It was annexed by the city of Hopewell in 1923 but earlier served as headquarters of the Union Army during the Siege of Petersburg during the American Civil War.]

Alma (left) at home in City Point, Virginia, 1915, with Mom & Dad and young Methodist minister.

It was giving over our spare bedroom to the young Methodist minister and his wife whose house was not yet finished.

It was taking piano lessons at Miss Mary's, where a carefully preserved bloody footprint on a panel of the wall was an insistent reminder that this very place had been a battlefield in the War Between the States.

It was being left in the custody of a big-bosomed black woman while my parents visited Grant's breastworks, the Cavern of Luray and other points of interest.

Mother made a lot of new friends, learned to play bridge and went dancing at the clubhouse. Daddy reluctantly agreed to make a fourth at bridge and accompanied her to the clubhouse, but he never learned to dance. They both sang in the Methodist church choir. Then in a matter of months, we were headed back to New Jersey, all together this time on the train. Because ostensibly I was in her charge, our colored maid was permitted to ride in the Pullman car.

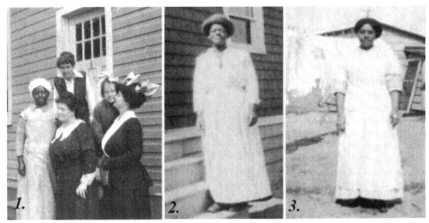

1. Ida (l.), Alma & Mom (r.) 2. Henrietta 3. Ida

Living quarters. Ida (left). Henrietta (right).

Daddy had been transferred to the company's plant **[pds: Plant No. 1 – the Smokeless Powder Works]** at Carney's Point, New Jersey, less than a hundred miles from our home in Cedarville but light years away. Again we lived in a supervisor's village, the two-story houses adequate, but without the ambience to which we had become accustomed.

> **[ARJ: "We took a black girl with us who became our live-in maid. Although Daddy worked at Carney's Point, we lived in nearby Pennsville, N.J. My Uncle Clarence and his wife, Mable, also lived**

in Pennsville and he was a top mechanic at the motor pool."]

Mother soon was deeply involved in Red Cross work and Liberty Bond drives and in knitting khaki sweaters "for the boys." Daddy was heard telling someone that she even took her knitting to the bathroom, a joke which offended her sensibilities. He never told it again.

I remember the place as muddy and cold and boring. To break the monotony, my friend Alice and I thought up stunts like walking on the frozen Delaware river, jumping from one cake of ice to another like Eliza in *Uncle Tom's Cabin* and playing "Follow the Leader" with the boys down the street, which often included climbing up and over a regiment of boxcars parked on a railroad siding. I never told Mother about these escapades. She tried hard to bring me up to be a lady.

The one shining never-to-be-forgotten happening of that long cold winter was the arrival of a set of Compton's Pictured Encyclopedia just for me. I lifted them carefully from their stout wooden crate and without interruption except for meals, turned every page in every book until I had reached the last page of volume twenty.

I repacked them myself when we suddenly left The Company – and the maid – behind and moved into a house near East Lake in Bridgeton, county seat of Cumberland County and only a dozen miles from Cedarville. And when we moved to a smaller house in a less fashionable neighborhood, and when we stored our things and moved in with the widow next door. All in less than two years.

I never asked why and I was never told, but I saw my father kneeling in front of an open window one night, gasping for breath and somehow I knew that his heart was "bad", that the doctor had said he could never work again, but that he was determined to find something he could do and that his sometimes week-long absences from home were in search of that something. I understood that our lovely home in Cedarville had been sold.

[ARJ: " In 1917 or 1918 Daddy suddenly almost died of a heart attack and was told he could never work again. Mother and I lived in a rented duplex in Bridgeton and I walked across town to school (fifth grade). I never knew why we moved there or where Daddy was or what really happened. At our house nothing except maybe the weather was discussed 'in front of the child.' As 1 told Aunt Alma years later, I might as well have been brought up in a closet. Nobody ever told me anything or even hugged or kissed me, except

Aunt Alma. The conversation was supposed to be for adults and
nobody was allowed to touch me for fear I'd get germs. Nobody
actually disliked me, although 1 think kids drove my Dad crazy, they
partly were doing what they thought best for me and partly they
were just busy with their own affairs. But I felt pretty lonesome
sometimes."]

Mother spent a lot of time visiting her two elderly and ailing aunts who
lived in town and in playing solitaire. What with walking a mile each way to
school, doing my homework and practicing on the piano every day, and with
terrifying suddenness "becoming a woman", I gave little thought to the war.
Neither of us really noticed when the armistice was signed.

[ARJ: "Eventually Daddy was allowed to look for a job that would
keep him outdoors and carried no stressful responsibilities. He
became a time-keeper in the growing fields at the Seabrook Farms
and we moved out there, six miles north of Bridgeton."]

4 – SEABROOK FARMS, NEW JERSEY

Another new house in another supervisors' village, but this time I loved it. The settlement was carved out of an alfalfa field, long rows of feather-topped carrots stretched out across the road in front of us, and just next to the left were acres of strawberries under an innovative overhead irrigation system. Down the road was a moist woodland where violets and honeysuckle grew. My new Airedale and I explored every inch of it.

View of Seabrook Farms, Bridgeton, N. J.

We had moved out to the Seabrook Farms just in time for me to start high school. We were six miles from town so I had to ride the school bus but I continued classes with my old school friends. Perfect.

Mother settled in surprisingly well. Soon after our arrival she was asked to act as temporary replacement at the office when the telephone switchboard operator was ill, discovered that she enjoyed the job and became a permanent employee before the year ended.

Daddy's supervisory position entailed driving daily over most of that vast acreage in a little horse-drawn buggy, punching time cards and making sure the field hands were where they were supposed to be. Being outdoors all day and under no strain did wonders for his health and when the new cold storage plant became operational, he was put in charge. Two years later he was given the added responsibility of supervising shipment over the newly constructed private railroad siding.

Being an only child, always the youngest in my class because of Mother's earlier pre-school tutoring, and deprived of the ordinary camaraderie between classmates by having to arrive and depart from school when the bus did, I seemed fated to be a perpetual innocent, not quite of this world, an incurable romantic. Living miles from the nearest member of my peer group did nothing to counteract this tendency. I thought I would like to become an artist or a poet but soon discovered I couldn't draw and my poems attracted no one's attention.

I started designing my own clothes, and making them. Except while we were contributing to the war effort, Miss Tompkins spent a week with us each spring and fall, refurbishing Mother's wardrobe. She had a sharp tongue and pasty white hands and scattered pins around like a shower of rain. When I was small, she paid me a penny for every ten I picked up. From breakfast to suppertime, the treadle machine never stopped whirring. Miss Tompkins didn't intentionally teach me to sew but I was interested and I paid attention. I made most of my clothes for the rest of my life.

Mother hoped I would become a musician. I was already a good accompanist at the age of fourteen. The little church down the road had an exceptionally good choir and I was drafted to play the organ. [**"at the local Episcopal Church, where I also went to Sunday school and Epworth League or Christian Endeavor or whatever."** – *letter to ed. from Alma, 18 July 1976.*]

We were once invited to sing on the air, making the 120-mile round trip to the radio station in Philadelphia by chartered bus. But as a musician I was not a social success. Popular music wasn't my bag and most kids my age didn't dig classical.

The road passing our house was paved one spring and was closed to all but local traffic for several months. The new pavement was perfect for skating. I wore out a good pair of steel-wheeled skates before the summer ended.

It was on that same stretch of road that I first drove a car. Truck, really. Model T. Built like a light farm wagon without shafts for a horse. A bright red little beauty, it belonged to a young man [**pds: Joe**] at a farm down the road where I went for milk every evening. I kept begging him to let me drive until he finally said if I could start it I could drive it.

He went in to supper one evening before I started home with the milk. The truck was backed into a shed between the house and the barn, the crank hanging there like an open invitation. I cranked it, it started, I jumped into the driver's seat and started down the drive. Joe exploded out the back door, climbed over the tailgate and sat down beside me. We rode decorously down to the crossroad, turned and came back. He never said a word.

I never had a yen to drive a motorcycle, although I rode in one often enough, in the sidecar. Vince, one of my schoolmates, had the rural delivery route for the *Bridgeton Evening News* and delivered the paper via motorcycle. His father borrowed the vehicle  on Friday nights to take two other girls and me to choir practice. We squeezed in somehow. On cold nights it was best to be on the bottom.

Mr. Shawn was treasurer of the Company and also a talented musical

Typical motorcyle and sidecar of the 1920s.

director. Under his supervision we gave some outstanding performances. It all fell apart when he suddenly moved his family to the state of Washington, reportedly because he was suspected of embezzlement. I'm sure Vince never suspected.

5 – BELFORD

The dances were held upstairs over the produce-packing shed in back of the boss's house. Once a month, one of the big storerooms was cleared out, the floor was waxed and the Company hired a band. Everybody came, arriving in time to listen to the musicians tuning up and staying until the last sweet notes of "Three O'clock in the Morning."

After the band went home, the whole world was hushed. I don't remember ever hearing a sound at night except an occasional hoot owl. I suppose that's why the boss **[pds: C.F.]** liked to live where he did, in the old family home with its trees and flower beds and old-fashioned grape arbor. An oasis in the bustling business center in daytime, a quiet Eden after dark.

The main office was just across the way in line with three or four houses built for the supervisors before the operation started to expand. The big platform scale took the center of the square, next came the cold storage plant and a long row of greenhouses where cucumbers climbed to the ceiling and various experiments were conducted. The garage was behind the packing shed then came a series of sheds where the mechanized farming equipment and a small fleet of Model T's was sheltered. There were also a machine shop and a carpenter's shop. The barn housing the last of the equine contingent was over on the far side, downwind. A cannery was added in 1922. Twenty years later Seabrook Farms was to begin processing and marketing its own brand of frozen foods and ultimately became the largest such operation in the world.

When we lived on the farm our village was separated from the business center by a mile of cultivated fields, the peach orchards were just beginning to bear and the latest experiment was a plantation of tulips intended to supply a mail order business and fresh blooms for markets in Philadelphia. The bulbs were imported from the Netherlands along with a corps of fresh-faced young men who were to oversee their acclimatization. Tubfuls of tulips in mouth-watering colors bedecked the room for the spring dance in April and the fox-trot and camel-walk were side-tracked to make room for gyrating couples waltzing "Dutch-style." The boys with the delightful accents and strange-sounding names like Hans and Huib became the nucleus of a busy round of parties involving all the girls in the surrounding area, and the social whirl subsided only when, inevitably, they all paired off. All but me.

Belford Seabrook, the boss's oldest son, happened to be just my age and the only other member of my class in the school bus. It seemed ordained that we should become a twosome and gradually I became like one of the family. Mrs. Seabrook drove Belford and me to the football games, to an occasional party, sometimes to the movies in her Model A sedan. C.F. (no one called Mr. Seabrook anything else) traveled all over the country in his Packard roadster, chauffeur driven. But there were times when we all – the two oldest Seabrook boys and their sister and I – piled into the big Packard, two of us sitting on the folding seats, and C.F. himself took us on a real outing.

Like the day at Atlantic City. We kids in rented suits dunked ourselves in the ocean and buried each other in the sand. Then, with Mrs. Seabrook, we joined C.F. who took us all to the dog races, the city's newest attraction. Later there was some sort of cocktail party in a hotel lobby at which Belford and I were served drinks. We accepted them graciously, then snickered as we surreptitiously "watered" the potted palms.

Clockwise (from left) – Alma and the Seabrooks: Thelma, Courtney, Belford.

Sometime before dinner, Belford and I walked to the north end of the boardwalk where a little amphibian biplane was tied at the end of a pier out beyond the breakers. The pilot, in puttees, gave us cotton to stuff in our ears then a padded helmet that buckled under the chin. Not too gracefully we boarded the plane and sat behind the pilot like three peas in a pod. With a roar, deafening in spite of the ear-covering, the little craft lurched out to sea then rose and headed south. We paralleled the boardwalk to the city limits, turned inland and followed Atlantic Avenue tack to our starting place. It took all of five minutes. For another five dollars, we had passport-sized pictures taken of both of us wearing our helmets.

Alma Henderson Duffield   **Belford Lawrence Seabrook (sans helmet)**

Toward the end of our junior year Belford got his driver's license, but it made little difference, he didn't have a car. C.F. believed each son should make his own way, as he had. If he wanted a car, he'd have to save for it. Belford worked hard every summer and was to become a successful and wealthy man, but not in the world of agriculture. It was John, the baby of the family, who "took after" his father, the man reputed to have "the green thumb of a Burbank and the business acumen of a Rockefeller". **[pds: John, also called "Jack", was born in 1917.]**

C.F.'s insistence on business before pleasure was responsible for the first of a series of incidents that were to change the course of our lives. He had invited an out-of-town business associate to spend the weekend and the man brought along his wife and daughter, my age. It happened to be the weekend of our monthly dancing party so C.F. proposed they attend en masse, Belford to be the daughter's escort. Ever the pragmatist, Belford courteously obliged.

I couldn't accept it. Belford and I were essentially friends, rather than lovers, but we had been a twosome for a long time. Our friends took it for granted that some day we would marry. And so did we, although we didn't talk about it often. We had a year of school to finish then four years of college. At least Belford had.

Before school started that fall, my parents, with no preliminary discussion, as was typical, had informed me that they could not afford to send me to college. I would go to Normal School and become a teacher. (If you contracted to teach two years after graduation, tuition was free.)

Bridgeton H.S. Senior Prom 1924

And there was more. A "reorganization" of the Company was taking place and it was rumored that a "management team" from New York was about to take over. **[ARJ: "During my final year, Seabrook went bankrupt, everybody was laid off."]** The strain was too much for my father. Soon after Christmas he and my mother moved to Paulsboro where he had found a stress-less job with the Mobil Oil Company.

I was shipped back to Bridgeton to live with family friends until I had finished high school.

6 – COLLEGE, LOVE AND CHARLES

No supervisor's village this. An ugly house on an ugly street in an ugly little town. The only salutary circumstance as far as I was concerned was the fact that the railroad station was just a short block from the house. When I heard the train coming I put down my cereal spoon, grabbed my school books and just made it to the station as the last car pulled away, the conductor standing on the rear platform to haul me aboard before the train picked up speed.

A short run, a change of trains – and direction – and a short walk brought me to the New Jersey State College at Glassboro [pds: **Glassboro Normal School**], a name to be heard round the world forty-three years later when President Johnson and Soviet Premier Kosygin held a summit meeting on the college campus. Ours was only the second class to be graduated. The campus was beautiful, the building smelled of new plaster. I felt as though I'd been sold down the river.

What they taught us, logically, was how to teach. How to make a "native" village in a sandbox with clay and cut paper and little sticks. I was all thumbs. How to teach tiny tots jolly little songs. My throat closed up. How to build a fire in a coal stove in case you had to teach in a little red schoolhouse. All the schoolhouses I had seen were built of red brick, had at least twelve rooms and had a furnace installed in the basement.

But morning assembly made up for the rest. The whole student body filed into the big auditorium. Everyone saluted the flag, recited the Lord's Prayer and the superintendent made a few remarks. Then came the songs, accompanied by me, sitting at the beautiful, big concert grand piano and putting body and soul into playing it. I also played for the Glee Club.

[pds: **The Glee Club was one of the most popular organizations on the school. Composed of 125 students, it met every Thursday afternoon under the leadership of musical director Miss Florence C. Dare. Alma Duffield was the assistant accompanist under accompanist Dorothy Baker. In a short time, Alma became President of the organization.**]

[pds: **From the 1926 college yearbook** *The Oak*: **"During the Easter vacation the members of the club visited the Home for Crippled**

Children in Philadelphia. They entertained the children with some delightful songs and dramatized the story of the Fairy Opera, 'Hansel and Gretel.' The enthusiastic youngsters were each presented with a daffodil, and showed their appreciation by playing their harmonicas."]

Alma Duffield ↑

[pds: During the year 1923-1924, Alma became treasurer of the Omega Delta Literary Society whose purpose was to "open the door to those who have a desire for knowledge. That year the Society 'received the second prize, a sum of thirty-five dollars, awarded by Mr. Synott for special achievement of literary societies.'"]

ALMA HENDERSON DUFFIELD
Paulsboro
"Duff"

Organizations—Omega Delta, Music Club, Glee Club.

Offices—President Glee Club, Orchestra Accompanist Glee Club, Assistant Treasurer Omega Delta.

"By music mind as equal temper know,
Nor swell too high, nor sink too low."

The school greatly appreciates Alma's musical and executive work in the Orchestra, Glee and Music Clubs. Besides contributing much to our entertainment, she has helped us in numerous other ways, especially in her dependable work on committees. May your artistic temperament always gain for you as many admirers as it has in G. S. N. S.

After graduation when I became responsible for teaching the Three Rs to a roomful of noisy little wrigglers, I went home and had hysterics every night for a week. Life in Paulsboro wasn't all bad, however. I arrived in style, in a model A driven by a new friend, an engineer ten years older than I, whom I had met at one of the Company dances. He was the latest in a succession of new acquaintances I had made while living in Bridgeton, after having firmly told Belford never to darken my door again.

Glassboro Normal Orchestra - 1926

I never have decided whether my engineer's intentions were "good" or otherwise, but he took me to my first musical comedy, told me I had interesting idiosyncrasies, and said that if I was to become a writer (my latest ambition) I needed to first learn more about life.

He deposited me and my luggage at my new home, paid his respects to my mother and we made a date for the following week. When he returned, Mother greeted him warmly. He said he'd planned to drive down to Greenwich where they were having some sort of celebration, and would she like to go? She said she would; we spent the evening as a threesome. I never figured that one out, but he never called again.

Fate decreed that I was not to languish alone, however. Almost immediately the girl next door invited me to join a "sorority", the sole purpose of which was to invite all the unattached young men in town to various picnics and parties. None of us, individually, would have had the audacity to ask a man for a date, but calling ourselves the Delta something-or-other – and stitching Greek letters on the bosoms of our bathing suits – made it all quite respectable.

We had indoor parties, dancing to the music of someone's Victrola (we were learning the Charleston). We had wiener roasts at night by the light of a bonfire on the beach, a narrow strip of sand by the river's edge, pleasant enough after dark except when there had been an oil spill at the refinery half a mile downstream. (I played the ukulele.) Sometimes we attended a show in Philadelphia, taking the train to Camden and crossing the Delaware by ferry. This necessitated taking the late train home much to the dismay of some of our parents, especially mine. And one memorable evening we enjoyed a cruise down the Delaware from Philadelphia, a trip which included dining and dancing and lounging in deck chairs, watching the shore lights drift by.

Of course we soon paired off. Charles ("Cully") Flowers and I were attracted to each other and soon we were dating. One night we went to see *The Phantom of the Opera*, a black and white film which played in one of Philadelphia's largest theaters and was accompanied by the thrilling music of a grand pipe organ. Later, at the same theater, we were amazed by the first talking picture, Al Jolson in *The Jazz Singer*.

Inevitably the fun and games ended and were followed by a succession of weddings. Although I was, as always, the youngest in the group and not actually "in love," I was extremely susceptible to the ambience. I decided I wanted to get married, too.

My parents objected, of course. They liked Charles. He was a nice boy and he had a good job. But they thought we were too young to be married. I thought otherwise. I was eighteen, a college graduate with a teaching contract, and felt capable of making my own decisions, but to keep the peace, I agreed to wait until my nineteenth birthday. Actually, we waited another nine days, until the day after Christmas, then went to New York City on our honeymoon and were in Times Square on New Year's Eve, I, nearly hidden under my ankle-length winter coat and my fashionable but graceless bell-shaped hat.

[pds: They were married on December 26, 1926 in the Trinity Episcopal Church, Camden, New Jersey.]

Meanwhile, ever the romantic, I wrote to Belford and agreed to meet him for a final farewell. We vowed never to forget each other and remarkably, we never did. We wrote to each other once a year and he came across the continent to see me twice, the last time, three years before he died at the age of seventy-three.

[pds: Before his first visit, Belford had served his country well, as reported by *The Examiner*, Launceston, Tasmania, Wed., November 29, 1944: "Importance attached to Tasmania as a source of food for Allied forces in the Pacific area is shown by the visit of high-ranking U.S. Army officers, who will spend several days in the state as part of a survey of Australian productivity. Col. Logan, Deputy-Director of Procurement for the U.S. Army, who has his headquarters at Washington, will arrive by air to-day and spend several days visiting Tasmanian berry fruit and vegetable growing areas in company with Major Belford L. Seabrook, in charge of the Agricultural Division of Procurement (U.S. Army), and Commonwealth food control officers. Major Seabrook in peace time was manager of the world's largest vegetable and berry farm, located in New Jersey, U.S. The farm comprised 33.000 acres of vegetables and 3000 acres of berry fruits."]

[pds: Belford, with his wife, the former Harriet Eakins, first visited Alma in 1951 when she lived in Oracle, Arizona. Harriet died in 1959. In 1960, he married Dorothea (?), but they divorced in 1970. Belford's second (and last) visit was in 1980. Belford brought his third wife, the former June Beatrice Weiss, for a dinner reunion at a local Nogales restaurant. – (From a letter written by Alma to son John Ready in October, 1996)]

[pds: On June 13, 1982, Belford died of brain cancer at his home in Arlington, Texas.]

Mother, as usual, had plunged full tilt into Paulsboro community affairs. In no time she became a member of the Methodist Church, sang in the choir, taught a Sunday school class, was president of the Women's Club and belonged to two bridge clubs.

I firmly declined to join a club, but before the year's end found myself taking pipe organ lessons on Thursday, playing at choir rehearsal on Friday, traveling to Philadelphia for a piano lesson on Saturday and playing the organ at church on Sunday morning. Mother's tendency toward over-achievement or kinetic behavior or whatever, was either hereditary or contagious.

Philip S. Duffield (1870-1967)   Ada Henderson Duffield (1884-1936)

I never understood my mother. I never really knew her. I don't think anyone did. Innately shy and perhaps oversensitive, her apparent friendliness and willingness to be of service were coupled with a certain naïveté and a quiet dignity which kept people at a distance. Since Cedarville I had never heard anyone call her by her first name. Now, I think her attitude probably was an unconscious way of concealing her true feelings. Although the course of her life must have differed greatly from her expectations, she never complained. My father had given her everything it was in his power to give, and had tried to protect her from life's buffets, perhaps over-protected her. I think she saw the world not as it was but as she thought it ought to be.

I had begun mistrusting her judgment when we lived on the Farm. She once refused to let me attend a football game because I would have to ride home with Ken, an obliging high school senior who thought of me as a silly kid. But she had no objections to my riding with one of the Company supervisors, a married man who always took the long way home and protested that he only wanted "a little feel." By the time we were settled in Paulsboro I had stopped listening to her advice altogether. My father and I had long since become strangers.

7 – FROM TEACHER TO HOUSEWIFE

So I was a schoolteacher, a student of music, a church organist, a married woman and a housewife. I was nineteen. The immediate problem was I didn't know how to cook. Evidently my mother hadn't felt cooking was a requisite skill for ladyship. But we had to eat and I tried.

Paulsboro's 14-room Billingsport Grade School, built in 1924, accommodated 438 pupils.

Charles was not helpful, but he was patient, as he was with my other deficiencies, up to a point. The point was reached when, without consulting him, I signed an easy-payment contract to buy a radio. It was a big, beautiful set with a built-in speaker, batteries included, and helped to furnish the room which was otherwise almost empty. But as Charles explained, it was the principle of the thing. Not only would it put us nearly a hundred dollars in debt but I should have discussed the purchase with him. Nor was it my first offense. I had spent my first paycheck – all of it – for a hand-painted dinnerware set from Czechoslovakia at the Sesquicentennial Exposition in Philadelphia.

Certainly I didn't know how to handle money. I had never had any to handle. Like Mother, Daddy was not dictatorial, but he made the decisions and paid the bills so Mother wouldn't have to worry her pretty little head about a thing. He even bought the groceries. Neatly lined up in our neat and clean basement in that faraway home in Cedarville, had been enough cases of canned fruits and vegetables to see us through the winter, ordered by Daddy from Sears and Roebuck. Since Cedarville he had made the weekly shopping trips. If some small extra was needed, I was sent to the corner store. I don't think Mother ever set foot in a grocery.

Now, I shopped and I cooked although I did send laundry out to be rough-dried. Ironing was done on Saturday along with cleaning the bathroom and kitchen and dusting and sweeping out the long hall of that unglamorous "railroad flat"; living room, two bedrooms, bathroom and kitchen lined up like boxcars on half the second floor of a homely frame building at the edge of town.

The Saturday piano lesson in Philadelphia had been canceled. There wasn't time. And I had begun to resent having to spend every Friday night and Sunday morning at the organ. I had disliked teaching in the beginning and I liked it no better as the second winter's weather grew colder. I seemed to spend more time getting the little wrigglers into their snow suits than in trying to explain that two and two always make four.

Teaching Grade One - 1926-1927

I quit. Right in the middle of the year. Contract or no contract. I cited "reasons of health". The superintendent jumped to the conclusion that I was pregnant and I let him think so. It was the only valid excuse for resignation. Married teachers had been acceptable for the last several years, provided they didn't smoke. Pregnant teachers, never.

Donald Crispin Flowers, born Jan. 9, 1930.

[Alma: "Then suddenly in the middle of my second year of teaching I blew it all. Quit teaching and playing and going to church and moved to another town and became a housewife and. was bored to death and a year later had a baby." - *letter to ed., 18 July 1976*]

We moved to Woodbury, eight miles inland from the river on the railroad's main line. An older and prettier town. Charles would commute by car with a friend who had preceded us. Our first floor apartment was one of four carved out of one of the old family homes. The living room had a bay window overlooking the tree-lined street. To get to the kitchen and dining alcove you paraded through the bedroom. The bathroom was tacked on behind.

I thrived on indolence. I joined a bridge club and began to find some pleasure in learning to cook. I made a friend of my husband's boss's wife who lived down the street. Then I got pregnant.

A new residential court opened up a few blocks away. It was modern, more convenient and not unattractive. It seemed expedient to move. We settled in just before the baby was born in January. We gave him the bedroom and slept on the Murphy bed in the living room.

The boss's wife thought the place would be too hot for a baby in summer. She suggested that when they left to spend the summer at her mother's home in Pennsylvania, we live in their house, rent free except for utilities and service of a gardener. They even allowed us use of a Model A. We rattled around in the big house but all the trees and greenery did make it cooler. I got a driver's license and seized every opportunity to drive the car. I also made myself at home in the library. It was an eclectic collection and motivated me to start thinking for myself, something two years at a teacher's college had failed to do.

Gradually I sorted out what I really believed and what I wanted to do with the rest of my life. I recognized that Charles and I were totally unsuited to each other and resolved to do something about it.

[Alma: **"When Don was a few months old I blew that too. Left him with my mother and went to Philadelphia and went to business college."** – *letter to ed., 18 July 1976*]

Peirce School of Business Administration

Courses of Study (university-grade) preparing young men and young women for the responsibilities of business life:

Business Administration
Accounting (C. P. A.)
Stenographic-Secretary
Executive-Secretary
Teacher-Training

Students Live in Private Homes with Proper Cultural Environment.

Sixty-second Catalogue upon application.

PEIRCE SCHOOL

Pine Street, West of Broad   Philadelphia

Surprisingly, the boss's wife came to my aid. She loaned me the money without interest to go to Peirce School of Business Administration in Philadelphia, to be paid back after I got a job. Mother agreed to take care of the baby. Charles had very little choice in the matter.

I learned to manage money in a hurry. My friend wisely advanced the loan in weekly installments. If I didn't stick to my budget I went to bed hungry on the night before "payday". I lived on North Broadway where room rents were low and ate at the automat. For recreation there was window-shopping, the Museum of Art, long walks in Fairmount Park and in summer the Philadelphia Orchestra's concerts under the stars. During the week you could see a good movie for twenty-five cents in the balcony.

I had intended to live with my parents and commute to the city but my father and I quarreled bitterly before the first week ended and I left for good. Mother said very little about the situation. She bundled it all inside, along with an accumulated mass of worry, hurt and disappointment which probably had already reached unbearable proportions. She quickly had become involved in civic affairs in her new home but she must have been keenly aware that the move from the Farm was another step in the downward spiral, that our ugly house was not just a stop-gap and that when Daddy accepted the "position" as a night-time switchboard operator at the oil refinery, he had reached the bottom of the barrel. **[pds: It was his last job.]** The biannual visits of Miss Tompkins, the prima donna of the sewing machine, were a thing of the past.

"Duffie"

[From MOBILIFE, December, 1954, a publication of Socony-Vacuum Oil Company, Paulsboro, New Jersey: "Phillip S. Duffield, who is 84, retired in 1941 after seventeen years service. He was first a checker in the Package Division. Because of his experience as a telegraph operator Phil was later made switch-board operator in the Main Office. Phillip was once ticket agent at the East Bridgeton office of the Jersey Central Railroad, on the Cumberland-Maurice River Branch. He learned his "dot-dash" at the Valentine Telegraph School in Janesville, Wisconsin. His instructor was George S. Parker, who had already invented the famous Parker Pen.]

As always, mother tried to save face, to transcend the unfortunate situation by being the perfect wife, mother and grandmother while at the same time, being the faithful member of the Methodist flock and the model clubwoman. But the flesh was weak. At the age of forty-six, she had a cerebral hemorrhage, the same thing that had caused her mother's death a few years earlier.

8 – SURVIVING THE GREAT DEPRESSION

The Great Depression meant different things to different members of my family. Luckily, neither my father nor my husband lost his job, and neither of them had anything else to lose. My father's savings were gone but since he never bought anything unless he had the cash to pay for it, he had no debts. Neither did we, thanks to Charles' good management. A car was considered a luxury which we couldn't afford. My father had never owned one.

After meeting the expenses incurred by Mother's illness – he had no medical insurance – my father was forced to retrench once more. He found a smaller house, a bungalow since Mother could no longer climb stairs, on an unpaved street near the edge of town. As a further economy measure, he had the telephone disconnected.

Mother now felt completely isolated. Further, she was entirely dependent on friends for transportation. Except for a weakness in one leg which made her afraid of falling, she had made a good recovery from the stroke, but she became increasingly despondent, her thoughts turned inward. Apparently to escape the present, she began to dwell in the past. At times, in writing one of her frequent letters, she confused me with her sister whose namesake I was.

Preoccupied with my own affairs, I was only vaguely aware of the situation at home. I had run out of money. At the Peirce school, each student advanced at his own speed and mine obviously was slower than I had expected. I was in desperate need of a job and less proficient than dozens of other job-seekers. But again I was lucky. The school took a remarkable personal interest in its students' welfare and when, in the midst of all this, Mother was stricken and I had to find a way to take care of the baby, they not only found me a job I could handle, but a baby-care facility, both within walking distance of the YWCA where I could live cheaply.

Charles was agreeable and willing to pay the baby-care expense. The establishment was a joint venture of two middle-aged widows who had converted the first floor of one of Germantown's big beautiful houses to accommodate a day-care center for pre-schoolers and a dormitory for five or six infantile "boarding students". The top two floors were divided into small apartments and single rooms.

Months later, when I had tired of the restrictive life in a YWCA, I moved into one of the third floor rooms. The others were occupied by a young insurance man and his wife who reportedly fed him entirely on canned soup; a talented portrait photographer who also constructed musical instruments from wood salvaged from old buildings, and his red-headed wife who painted exquisite miniatures. The room nearest mine was occupied by a young lawyer I seldom saw but who, at the suggestion of our landlady, protected my interests without charge when Charles decided to remarry and wanted custody of the baby.

Germantown YWCA building near Vernon Park
Photo: Flying Kite

[ARJ: "Don's father married an older woman who apparently regarded me as a hussy – I remember Don bawling me out for saying 'damn' once. Anyhow, for a long time I regarded all church-goers as a bunch of hypocrites. But of course that was just an immature reaction and I got over it in time. But I never became associated with the church again."]

My job was at the Germantown Cadillac-Lasalle agency where I operated the telephone switchboard and typed reports for the salesmen. For sixteen dollars per week. Which was on a par with most of the nineteen other girls who lived at the Y. The YWCA building, a white-pillared old mansion, sat behind a small park **[pds: Vernon Park]** which in better days had been part of an estate whose owners once had entertained General George Washington when he was president of the United States and Philadelphia was its capital.

The public rooms were beautifully furnished, the management friendly and the place was a haven for girls like me. Breakfast and dinner were included in the nominal room rent and if you were out of work, as I was a year later when General Motors cut the wages of every employee and I quit in a huff, rent was waived altogether until such time as you should be re-employed.

It was during the weeks of my unemployment that I gave some thought to the Great Depression. I did manage to get a job as a clerk in the Five and Ten Cent Store on Saturdays during the Christmas pre-holiday season. The two dollars I received was enough to pay for my subway fare downtown each weekday and for lunch at a drugstore counter.

Each morning began with a seemingly endless wait at one of the big employment offices. On good days I was sent out to be interviewed by a prospective employer, and some of the interviews were pretty weird, but eventually I got a job. In the beginning, I had hoped to work in a publishing house, but I soon learned that you didn't shop around, you said "yes" to the first person who offered to hire you. You didn't even ask what they'd pay. You just asked "When do I start?"

The person who hired me was a woman, the manager of a dining room catering to various women's groups. Each group was free to hold a business meeting or sell tickets for an entertainment. We charged a small fee for a reservation and provided a nicely served and tasty luncheon. The group's only obligation was to listen to the manager's spiel as she enumerated the superior qualities of each item on the menu. I acted as her secretary and after the meal, as sales clerk at our little retail shop in the back of the room. It was a clever scheme and quite successful, for a time.

Charles had married again and taken Donald to live in the suburbs, leaving me with visitation rights, but no alimony. Since I was working downtown, it seemed sensible to live downtown, so I took a third-floor apartment on Chestnut Street north of Broadway, one of those one-room affairs in which the "kitchen" consisted of a table and a two-burner gas plate and the privilege of washing dishes in the bathroom

It wasn't easy but I didn't mind because I had fallen in love.

9 – LOVE AND MARRIAGE – AGAIN!

Having somehow jumped from childhood to motherhood without committing most of the idiocies of adolescence I proceeded to make up for lost time. I decided that love was All.

The object of my affection was a musician named Sam **[pds: Samuel C. Walton]** who played a hot trumpet in a dance band – when they could get a job. We met on the subway while I was still in school; I would be coming home after a day at the typewriter and he would get off at the same station after spending the day in line at one of the employment offices, to appease his mother. Actually, as it turned out, if an interview appeared imminent, he graciously relinquished his place in line to some older man who "looked as though he needed a job."

His mother was a bit of a martinet, the widow of a Philadelphia cop who had been killed in action leaving her a small pension and top priority on the list of those eligible for the night-time job of cleaning at City Hall. Her oldest son had a steady job in a warehouse downtown, Sam's sister worked in a stocking factory, and both turned over their weekly paychecks rather than face mama's disapprobation.

But it was hard to be hard on Sam. Already playing trumpet in the school band at the age of eleven, he was the victim of an accident in a butcher shop and was missing one and a half fingers of his right hand. In spite of the handicap and encouraged by his physical therapist, he had become an excellent performer. To him, life was just a bowl of cherries He was good and he knew the band would eventually get another gig.

To me, it was an intriguing glimpse of another world. To Sam also, I think. But basically there was a strong physical attraction between us. Then there was my possibly subconscious search for guidance to life in the big city, and possibly his appreciation of a friendship freely offered and uncritical. We became inseparable.

We spent hours wandering in Fairmount Park, or if the weather was unaccommodating, drinking coffee at the automat. If the band had a Saturday night gig, I sat on the sidelines watching the dancers, and afterward we sat on a park bench and talked. (We girls at the "Y" circumvented the eleven o'clock curfew by making arrangements with the girl who roomed at the top of the fire escape.)

Sam and I made no plans, we took it one day at a time. On rare occasions, through Sam's "contacts," we were able to enjoy a real treat, like an evening in an out-of-the-way night club where the attraction was a recently discovered young trumpet player named Louis Armstrong. We got up before dawn to watch the circus unloading at a railroad siding. We went to the Zoo and the Art Museum and watched the boat races on the Schuylkill.

We rarely thought about money. Sam lived – and ate – at home. I had quit the Cadillac agency because my pay was cut from $16 to $15 per week and I never made more. But by moving downtown and walking to work I saved ten cents a day and besides food my only real necessity was shoes. I even squeezed out enough to buy a red scarf to wear with my gray winter coat. Sam said it made me look like a Main-Liner, a real compliment if you knew Philadelphia.

The winter coat – or rather lack of one – was almost my undoing. I was quite good at alterations and repairs and had managed to keep the rest of my wardrobe in decent shape. But I needed a warm coat and with neither money nor credit, faced a miserable winter. Finally I swallowed my pride and wrote to Mother's oldest brother. He sent me a check and told me to regard it as a gift, not a loan. I have never forgotten.

Sam's mother didn't like me. She couldn't forget that legally I was a married woman, and two years older than Sam. I think she thought I was trying to seduce him. Little did she know.

On one unforgettable afternoon I went to a neighborhood – Sam's neighborhood – dentist and had all four wisdom teeth removed. He gave me some cotton to stuff in my mouth and a shot of something to deaden the pain and bid me farewell. How I made it home I'll never know – with the help of more than one stranger, I'm sure – but I rode the trolley, transferred to the subway, then walked five blocks and upstairs.

Sam came over later to find me agonizing and nearly unconscious and called his mother to tell her he was staying all night. Before sun up next morning, after her nightly stint at City Hall, Mama sailed in with the wind behind her. I'd have been terrified if I had been conscious enough to care. I just pulled the covers up and shut my eyes and after a while she disappeared. Next day she sent a potted plant by way of apology. I let it die. We never learned to like each other.

Eventually her attitude started to irk us both and we began to talk about marriage. We were unable to set a date, however because Charles had agreed to arrange a divorce – and pay for it – only if I let him file the petition on grounds of desertion, thereby leaving his escutcheon unsmirched. I didn't care whether my escutcheon was smirched or not and he was the one with the check book. We waited.

President Calvin Coolidge reportedly said, "When more and more people are thrown out of work, unemployment results." I found this to be true. The dining-room-advertising-shop was bankrupt. I was thrown out of work. It was back to the employment office line.

Again I was lucky. One of the big department stores was hiring and I was taken on as one of half a dozen girls who sat in a room next to the room of the secretary to the president of the company, and operated a comptometer all day. I wasn't hired because I knew how to operate a comptometer – I learned that in a day – but probably because I spoke the King's English and was therefore a fitting subject to sit in such close proximity to the president's secretary.

10 – MY KALEIDOSCOPIC LIFE

Sam and I were joined in matrimony one Saturday afternoon **[pds: 1933]** by a Justice of the Peace in one of Philadelphia's suburbs. I can't remember which one. With our sole possessions – my suitcase, and I believe Sam carried a fabric overnight bag in addition to his trumpet case – we moved into Mrs. Gregory's boarding house. From our third floor bedroom window we could look across two rows of neat brick houses to the park and a glimpse of Independence Hall. Downstairs, with a handful of other roomers, we enjoyed a decent breakfast and a satisfying dinner at night.

Independence Hall from our window - 1933.

Living in a boarding house relieved me of the odious business of cooking dinner for two on a hot plate, but unless we had the price of a night on the town, and we seldom did, we were doomed to confinement in one small bedroom. This soon began to pall.

Only a few blocks away and still within walking distance of my job, we found a basement apartment in one of those converted brick homes on a quiet tree-shaded street where the gleaming front steps led directly from the pavement to the entrance hall and the steps to the basement led downward beneath the others. The place was decently furnished and comfortable. A window at eye level in the bedroom looked out on the street, another in the living room looked out on a small paved court and was the conduit for a regular early evening concert by a pianist on one of the upper floors. I always dropped everything to listen to his rendition of "Smoke Gets in Your Eyes".

I wasn't so happy with the situation at the store. The six of us added long columns of figures showing total receipts of each department for the day and compared them with like columns for each of the previous ten years. It was deadly dull but that isn't what set me fantasizing about being able to quit. Sheathed and constrained in a semblance of a less matronly figure, moving stiffly on stiletto heels, her thinning hair dyed a fashionable shade of auburn, and with a bright painted smile reserved for the president and his cronies, Madame Secretary supervised us peons with an insufferably arrogant air. I thought of her as a witch.

Happily, I was rescued by the manager of Ladies' Ready-to-Wear, who needed a secretary. Easy to work for, he was a round-faced, rather short person, bald as a billiard ball. Approaching middle age, he dressed well and lived well in a fashionable downtown apartment, taken care of by a Japanese manservant. He invited me to a dinner party one time, along with a lot of buyers and department heads. I enjoyed the conviviality and the conversation but was rocked back on my heels when I lost two-thirds of a whole week's pay with one toss of the dice in some sort of gambling game.

Employees of the company were allowed to charge purchases up to the amount of two weeks' pay, to be repaid at the rate of five dollars per week. This pseudo-generosity worked out very well – for the company. Almost no one could resist making a purchase or two, and repaying the five dollars out of a fifteen dollar pay check left barely enough for room and board. From that day forward, since you never had the cash to shop elsewhere, you were hopelessly shackled to the company store. The entire amount was due on the day you resigned. You couldn't even afford to quit.

There were advantages. One was the opportunity to belong to the chorus. Anyone who liked to sing was welcome and about 150 employees attended weekly rehearsals at which a well-qualified director prepared us for semi-annual concerts. The clincher was a free dinner preceding each rehearsal. The concerts were attended by a fashionable crowd and the proceeds donated to charity.

There were plenty of other things to do in the city, except on Sunday. Still in the grip of the "Blue Laws", everything was locked up tight and in good weather Fairmount Park was crowded. There was nowhere else to go, unless you took the bus which crossed the new Delaware Bridge to go to a movie in Camden, New Jersey.

There were occasional spectacles, priceless and free of charge, like the Mummers' parade on New Year's Day. We joined the wildly applauding but shivering spectators crushed shoulder to shoulder along Broadway. The crowd surged toward the street as each garishly costumed band came into view, but never broke ranks, marshaled as they were by the very appearance of the mounted policemen's horses side-stepping along the curb and presenting their iron-muscled glossy rumps at human eye-level.

Mummers Parade, circa 1920s

Typical Chinese New Year's Parade.

Half-frozen, we listened to a hundred tinkling tunes played by several hundred musicians on as many mandolins or banjos and a few ukuleles, while other members of each group, weighed down as they were by those outlandish costumes, performed intricate dances or marching routines. We stood our ground until the last gaudy group was out of sight.

I remember another New Year's Eve in an area of narrow streets. Dimlit and less crowded, the place had a foreign odor, faces were unfamiliar, sweetly haunting music pierced the darkness with strange harmonies. People leaned out of second- and third-story windows and dangled paper money tied to a string before the frightening jaws of a heaving and undulating huge paper dragon. Chinatown.

There were many things to remember, some I'd rather forget. Then as in a kaleidoscope, the picture changed. Sam's band had a new contract. Not for a series of Saturday nights, but for six nights a week for the fall and winter at a popular nightclub in Upstate New York. Sam left immediately. I spent a week there, in a hotel bedroom the size of a closet. I joined the others and listened to them talk shop at lunch time. During rehearsals I sat in a beer-scented bar-room and listened. In the evening I sat at a corner table and watched the dancers. I was glad to go home.

Our financial condition was much improved. I found I could afford to eat out every night, and once that became a habit, there seemed to be no reason for keeping the apartment. I moved into a room. The room was just around the corner in another of those remodeled three-story houses. Five or six of the other tenants ate at the same little Italian bar and restaurant and before long two tables in the far corner became the regular meeting place of our little group. One of the men had a car, so we pooled our money for gas and went to Atlantic City one Saturday afternoon, slept on the beach and came home on Sunday. We went to shows together. We had a lot of fun. I almost forgot I was married.

11 – ON THE ROAD: PHILADELPHIA TO SIDNEY

The band had another new contract, with a dance marathon promoter. They were opening in a rural area in New Jersey, central to several small cities. Sam insisted that I join them. I let myself be persuaded, partly, I suppose, because my conscience bothered me a little.

Members of the band were quartered in several private homes. Sam and I lived on a small farm with a middle-aged widow and her teen-age daughter. There was another boarder called Uncle Bill who kept a big touring car in the garage, jacked up and protected by a canvas cover. It was unwrapped only on very special occasions. The widow raised gladioli and other sturdy flowers as row crops in a field, and had an agreement with several local churches to keep their altars decorated. She also raised chickens.

The marathon tent seated about 750. The semi-circular dance floor, separated from the audience only by a rope barrier, curved around the bandstand and would accommodate ten or fifteen couples. Behind the band was a little auxiliary tent where the dancers, in rotation, could retire every hour for a ten-minute rest. A nurse was in attendance. Near the main entrance was the snack bar and the juke box which motivated the dancers when the band wasn't on duty.

As far as I know, the contest wasn't fixed. Most of the contestants were locals, but there had already evolved a handful of unemployed hopefuls who had learned a few tricks. When they had been eliminated from one contest, they quickly moved on to another, and there was little chance of a local winning the grand prize. I was too naive to understand much of what was going on, but I knew there was a lot of betting on the side and a lot of murmuring later in the city of Elizabeth when Dutch Schultz visited the scene. I wasn't really interested in watching one "dancer" drag another, asleep on her feet, around the floor. I was happier on the farm. I helped the widow cut flowers and pick cherries and was fascinated as an incubator full of eggs miraculously was transformed into a pen full of fluffy cheepers. Most of all, I enjoyed the company of the family dog, a Chow who thought he was a lap dog. He knew I liked dogs so every time I sat down, he leapt into my lap, pinning me down and completely obscuring the view. He made it up to me by taking me on long walks in the country.

Top: Dance marathon: event where people stay on their feet for a given length of time. Bottom: By the 1930s, dance marathons became a profitable business and participants who managed to make it to the end stood in line to win cash prizes.

It was while we lived at the widow's that Sam and I got enough money together to make a down payment on an automobile. A Buick roadster. Never mind that the canvas top was rotten, the leather seats cracked and the paint job almost kaput. The brakes weren't good for much either, nor the battery. We soon learned, when driving into town, to park at the top of a hill with the wheels toward the curb. When we were ready to leave, we hauled the wheel around and released the hand brake. By the time we had coasted to the bottom, the motor usually had caught and we were off.

It was by way of the car that I met Jim in Elisabeth where the marathon opened next. By that time I couldn't bring myself to watch – ever. We lived in a beautiful big room in a beautiful big house and spending an evening alone there really wasn't so bad. I found a lending library and started reading again. I also tried a little experiment. I had overheard some of the men talking about smoking "tea" (a now-forgotten name for "pot"). I rolled up a bunch of Lipton's in a cigarette paper and took a couple of puffs. End of experiment. Why anyone would want to do that, I couldn't imagine.

Sometimes I took the car out and cruised around town just for the pleasure of driving. I always stopped for gas at a nearby station and Jim was the man in charge. One day I asked him to check the battery – you had to add water every once in a while – which was under the floor board on the passenger side. When he attempted to replace it, the board wouldn't "sit" so he whacked it with a hammer and broke it in two. This struck us both as very funny and from then on we were good friends.

Formerly a copy writer at a prestigious advertising agency in NYC, Jim had buckled under the pressure and been advised by his psychiatrist to take a temporary outdoor job. We had endless discussions about writers and writing and he urged me to try writing again.

For a time, all my energy was directed elsewhere. Mother had suffered another stroke, her third, and this proved fatal. **[pds: Ada Duffield died at age 51 on May 7, 1936.]** I stayed to help my father for a while but as soon as he was able he retired to a little house in Cedarville where he was born.

Sam had stayed at his mother's after the show closed in Elizabeth. Now it was opening in New Bedford, Mass., and we joined it there. We spent the first nights in a little hotel on the waterfront where the second floor fire exit was a window in the hall. A thick rope coiled on the floor beneath it was attached to the wall under a sign which read, "In case of fire, throw the rope out the window and lower yourself knot by knot."

Later we found another of those "apartments" converted from a big bedroom in a big house where you cooked on a hot plate and washed dishes you know where. Luckily we had a room overlooking a quiet street lined with other big houses, each with a walled garden around it and a widow's walk on top. The frozen snow never thawed. From our windows we could watch people slipping and sliding and sometimes falling down. No wonder few people made the trip to the out-of-the-way amusement park to watch the marathon.

I ventured outdoors once in a while. I visited the fascinating Whaling Museum, admired the sculpture in front of city hall depicting "A Dead Whale or a Stove Boat", and watched the flotilla of gulls rocking gently in the midday sun on Buzzard's Bay. Mostly I practiced writing as Jim had suggested, tried to keep warm and waited for the marathon to fold. It didn't take long. I had a feeling that frigid weather and Great Depression aside, New Englanders weren't foolish enough to spend good money to watch a few zombies stumbling around a dance floor.

"A Dead Whale or a Stove Boat" sculpture in front of New Bedford's Public Library, quoting Captain Ahab from Herman Melville's novel Moby-Dick."

The band's summer job in a resort hotel in the Adirondacks was like a pine-scented paradise after purgatory. They needed a waitress and because they were desperate, agreed to give me the job. The band, and I, worked only in the evening except on weekends. It was almost like a paid vacation.

However, there was no longer doubt in my mind that love was not "All". It was of much less importance to me than a lot of other things, like a weekly pay check and an address other than General Delivery. When the season closed and the band departed, I stayed in the mountains. When the hotel closed, I worked at a hunting lodge. After hunting season, I traveled to a small town in Upstate New York **[pds: Sidney]** where one of the hunters **[pds: Raymond Simpson]** had told me there were jobs to be had.

Campbell Inn, Roscoe, New York (from 1924 postcard).

[pds: Trombone player Raymond Simpson, father of editor Patrick Simpson, played in a resort band at Campbell Inn, a Catskill summer resort in Roscoe, New York. From Campbell Inn's 1924 brochure: "As a fine orchestra is employed, dancing may be enjoyed each evening...The village (Roscoe) theatre presents 'talkies' and other attractions of an especially high order."]

The Depression, iron-fisted in the cities and in some rural areas, handled most small towns more gently. Sidney was a gray little town, now dependent on the magneto factory as it once had been on the railroad yard. But I found work and a decent apartment and began to feel like a person again.

12 – THIRD MARRIAGE – NOT THE CHARM ?

Raymond Simpson and his trombone, Sidney, N.Y., 1920.

My job at the factory was in Quality Control, sorting screws. If I found one with a burr on it, I tossed it in a separate bin to be reworked. My father never knew. He had been horrified when I was offered a job as a waitress while I was staying with him after Mother died. Said she would have considered it a disgrace and offered to give me an allowance instead. When he actually started to cry, I accepted it. Now I simply told him I had a steady job. But I had to tell him that Sam and I were separated, which was bad enough. Two divorces were unthinkable. And he kept reminding me that I "wasn't getting any younger." I was twenty-nine years old.

Sidney Magneto Plant, Sidney, N.Y. - 1936

Raymond was one of the men I had met at the hunting lodge. He had recently been divorced in New York City **[pds: no children]** and returned to his hometown to assist his father in the grain and feed business, He wanted a home of his own and two sons. I wanted security. It seemed a fair enough exchange. The hidden reef was the fact that we didn't really know each other.

Before we were married we hadn't discussed money and when Ray brought home his first check I assumed it was for two weeks pay. When a second check didn't appear on schedule, I learned that he was receiving one hundred dollars per month. His father, a tight-fisted little man who wore

overalls and worked in the store like a hired hand, had given the prodigal son a job with room and board and use of the company truck and pocket money besides. He evidently thought that was enough.

Ray's parents: Jay C. Simpson & "Mom," (a.k.a. Mary or "Mamie") Simpson (nee Shaw).

He and Mom and the hired girl lived in Mom's rooming house adjacent to the feed store, the whole complex nudging the railroad tracks at the foot of Main Street.

Dad did loosen up a little when I became pregnant. He offered to help Raymond build

Rooming house at 4 West Main Street, Sidney, New York.

a house, a cabin, really, one room and a portico with one end partitioned off into a kitchen and a bathroom with a chemical toilet. Dad was a good carpenter and the cabin was snug, built on a hillside on an abandoned farm he had picked up at a tax sale.

Meadowland sloped down to the forest on three sides. The view was soul-stretching. Behind us the road – just a track, really – continued half a mile to a rambling, weather-beaten house where two elderly, reclusive brothers eked out a living. They were to be my only neighbors for nearly three years.

I learned that my acquaintances felt sorry for me, "Living way out there." I loved it. I took long walks across the meadow and into the woods. Among other treasures in the forest I found arbutus, that tough little plant with the tiny pink blossoms whose heavenly scent took me back to my childhood. From the portico I watched deer bounding over the fences to browse in the derelict apple orchard. When the snows came, Raymond commuted in the truck, leaving it at the bottom of the non-negotiable hill and walking the last half mile. Our car was parked there too, in case I should ever need to get out.

After Pat was born [pds: Oct. 29, 1938], Dad added a little

Alma, with husband Ray Simpson and son Patrick - 1939.

bedroom at the back of the house. I built a rock garden around a lily pool made of an old washtub, and some sort of singing frog came to live there. I tried a garden but gave over to the rabbits. Wild strawberries and blackberries were free for the picking.

Pat was a happy, burbling baby, but Jimmy **[pds: James Edgar Simpson, born June 24, 1941]**, who arrived about a year later, was always complaining. The place wasn't big enough for the four of us, or really safe, either. Expecting me to cope with two babies in an emergency in such isolation wasn't realistic.

Left: Jimmy. **Right: Pat and father, Ray.**

We found a house in Unadilla ten miles from Sidney on the Susquehanna River, that river about which a Pennsylvanian, trying to sell land in London in 1794, reportedly remarked that its beauty was "excessive" and that it was secure from hostile Indians. Still true. The house was one hundred years old but in good shape, and had a little addition on one side in which lived a widow, a long-time tenant. I persuaded my father to loan us the money for a down payment.

Back in civilization, we began to feel the influence of a world at war. The factory had received a defense contract and was advertising for help. Raymond became a lathe operator and I planted a Victory Garden. We collected scrap iron and saved aluminum foil and I canned, preserved and pickled. I also hoed and weeded and cooked and cleaned and took care of two active little boys. I developed chronic sinusitis and laryngitis and bronchitis. The doctor suggested a milder climate.

13 Fellows Street
Unadilla, N.Y.

Unadilla - Pat and Jim - 1943

Because Raymond was exempted from the "peacetime" draft as a worker in a defense plant, he had to have permission from his employer to leave his job. Armed with such a certificate and another from my doctor affirming that the move was indicated by the state of my health, Raymond drove a truck loaded with what we considered essential. I drove the car with the boys and a dog **[pds: an Airedale named Taffy]** and we headed west on the highway.

[pds: Distances were great and they would need a lot of gas to get to Arizona. But since the onset of World War II, the government had found it necessary to ration food, gas, and even clothing. Americans had to apply for books of ration coupons, issued by the Office of Price Administration (OPA). A gas coupon, when torn off in the presence of the retailer, was good for only so many gallons of gas for a fixed period of time. Then you had to get more coupons; No coupons? No gas.

How my parents obtained enough gas coupons and money to get them clear across the country in two gas-guzzling vehicles during wartime has always been a mystery to me.]

Circa 1943: Raymond and the boys ready to leave for Arizona in their fully-loaded 1934 Ford Model BB truck, with Pat's pedal car atop the roof. (None of them look happy to be leaving.)

Right: Stopping for gas somewhere along the way. Alma is driving the 1939 Chevrolet 2-door sedan with the two boys and Taffy (the dog). (Pat's pedal car is still atop the truck.)

"Taffy, I've a feeling we're not in New York State any more."

After listening to a friend's account of a vacation in Arizona, I had become bewitched with the idea of living there I persuaded Raymond that Tucson, Arizona was the only place to consider. And luck was with us. He quickly found a job and to me the desert was a dream come true. I spent hours sunning the cold out of my bones and the boys played outdoors all day.

Pat's pedal car (above) makes its way safely to its new home, a duplex somewhere in Tucson, as Pat tries out his new scooter.

Raymond was unhappy. He was homesick and he didn't like the weather. He missed hunting and fishing in familiar country. It became obvious that if forced to choose between his home state and me, the choice wouldn't be me.

[pds: On a postcard to his mother from what was most likely their first trip to Nogales together, Raymond wrote:

> **"Nogales, Mexico, Thursday.**
> **Dear Mother,**
>   **Well, here we are – Pat, Jim, Alma and I down in**
>   **Mexico and we can't speak a word of 'Mexican'.**
>   **Having dinner in 'The Cave', a high class joint.**
> **Love to all,**
> **Raymond.]**

We made a deal. Since I was not physically capable of undertaking a new career and caring for two children at the same time, he would take the boys back to New York where his mother would care for them. I would take a refresher course and a civil service exam and go back to work. At the end of a year we would get together and decide what to do next.

I took the train for Colorado Springs and the rest of the family drove back to New York

13 – FOURTH MARRIAGE, FOURTH CHILD

I was still attending classes and living in a rooming house in downtown Colorado Springs when Raymond appeared with the boys in tow. He never explained then or later. The landlady said he identified himself, was told I was out, and left. Apparently he started back to New York the same day.

A few months later he did it again. I introduced him to the landlady, we had dinner together and the next day he was gone. This was a different landlady and my "home" was a basement apartment, a slight improvement over the room downtown, because now I was working.

I was a typist in Air Force Intelligence. But I didn't last long. I couldn't keep my mouth shut. Not that I blabbed any state secrets but I told my boss what I thought of the situation when one of the sergeants was demoted when he made what seemed to me a slight mistake. It was suggested that I transfer out to Camp Carson. I was delighted. I was hired as secretary to the boss of the whole shebang. Well, one third of the whole shebang. I promoted myself to a still better apartment, above ground.

[pds: Camp Carson (about 10 miles south of Colorado Springs) was established in 1942, following Japan's attack on Pearl Harbor. During World War II, over 100,000 soldiers trained at Camp Carson. It was also home to nearly 9,000 Axis prisoners of war – mostly Italians and Germans.]

The Reconditioning Center at Camp Carson was a grand experiment. There were three sections, the Hospital, the Physical Reconditioning Center and the Educational Reconditioning Center directed by my boss, a Captain in the nearly defunct U.S. Cavalry. His assistant was an Army Lieutenant, and he chose as the man to organize the school itself, an Air Force Colonel. The outfit prided itself on its utter disregard of rank and service organization and it worked out surprisingly well.

In Educational Reconditioning we started with several acres of empty barracks and a board full of keys. When we folded some two years later, we were operating a school where returning GIs could take anything from the basic three Rs to college credit courses or practical work in agriculture on a fifty-acre farm. The staff, including military and civilian, totaled 150.

My new apartment was in a converted small hotel in the heart of town near city hall. In the hotel, two rooms had shared a bathroom, now the apartments did the same thing. When you weren't using it, you just kept the door locked on your side. The tenants also shared the medicine cabinet and because a shaving outfit sat below my tooth brush, I assumed that my neighbor was a man. I never saw him.

When Raymond and the boys turned up for the third time, I made room for them and started looking for larger quarters. Raymond said he wanted to stay and actually started looking for a job. I took a day off and was able to get permission from the school superintendent to enroll the boys for the coming fall session in a residential area. When I got home that afternoon, they had disappeared again.

This time I asked for help and was advised by a lawyer who was a friend of a friend that I should file for divorce and ask for custody of the children. Getting the divorce was no problem, but it did take time. Meanwhile I met Ted.

[ARJ: "I know practically nothing about Teddy's background except that he was adopted by John Marshall Ready and Zura Mae Ullom of Sidney, Nebraska when he was a very small child. The Readys were ranchers and had four nearly grown daughters when they apparently picked Teddy up off the street after he had been abandoned or neglected by his natural father. The man was an immigrant from Sweden who had married a woman whose father was a German and her mother a Sioux Indian. His last name was Sandine. (I never knew his first.) For some reason Ted and his brother and two sisters were scattered and each was brought up by a different foster family. They never kept in touch."]

Ted [pds: Theodore Godfrey Ready] was a patient at the Reconditioning Center awaiting his final discharge from the Army. He was from the Nebraska Panhandle. He suggested that we go to New York, retake the boys and bring them up on a ranch in Nebraska. When he got his discharge and the Center started to fold, I agreed.

My boss reminded me that the Center treated two kinds of patients, those with trench foot and those with psychoneuroses. Ted didn't have trench foot. But he appeared normal to me and I always had unshakeable faith in my completely unreliable intuition.

Ted suggested that things would go forward faster if we set up housekeeping in Nebraska and actually got married when my interlocutory divorce became final three months later. I agreed, got pregnant on the first night in our new home, and a week later discovered that he already had a wife, right there in Scottsbluff County.

I had given up my job, spent all my savings on furnishings for the empty house Ted's boss had provided, was stranded on an isolated ranch in what might as well have been a foreign country, had no one to turn to. I did the only thing I could think of to do. Nothing.

Ted's wife gave him a divorce and he found another job. The house was a so-called basement house, not uncommon in the area. Only a few small windows and the roof were visible above ground. After Johnny was born and we kept two goats, we could hear them trit-trotting over the house-top in the moon light.

When I was six months pregnant, we finally made the trip to New York to get the boys. We bungled badly. A school-bus driver became suspicious when he noticed our Nebraska plates, alerted a teacher who called the police, and we almost landed in jail.

Ted had to return to his job in Nebraska. I stayed with friends to petition the court for custody. Not being able to afford anyone better, I retained a young and inexperienced lawyer. Raymond's mother had always been kind, but when the chips were down she sided with you know who. She bought the District Attorney.

I learned that Raymond's earlier divorce had prohibited him from re-marrying in New York State, which is why he had insisted that we be married in Pennsylvania. My divorce from Sam hadn't become final until three months after I married Raymond. The judge said my divorce in Colorado was not valid in New York State. Raymond testified that I had been living with a man in Colorado Springs, he knew because he had found the man's shaving things in my bathroom.

The judge gave Raymond an annulment and custody of the boys.

[ARJ: "He, the judge, thought a ranch in Nebraska, especially someone else's ranch, wouldn't be a good home for them."]

14 – FROM HEARTBREAK TO HARDSCRABBLE

While Johnny was still an infant, Ted's boss laid him off for the summer, and we moved to a ranch which was operated the year round. Our little house was located in the boss's backyard, the usual place. Hired help in the Panhandle were treated like second-class citizens. Not surprising, I suppose in an area where most of the ranchers had only recently been treated as second-class citizens themselves, "Polacks" and "Roosians".

Ranch life: Johnny, Alma and Ted.

Ted had said that by renting a ranch for two years, a good operator could accumulate enough to buy a ranch of his own. We found that since the war ended there were no ranches to rent or to buy. The veteran could work for somebody else, or else.

Ted didn't mind too much, he was out in the fields all day – area ranchers raised mostly beans and sugar beets, not cattle – but I soon had enough of being the hired help's helpmeet, having no door in the bedroom doorway, having to use an outdoor privy. When I complained that there was running water in the barn but none in our house, the boss very generously ran a line from the pump and up through a hole in the kitchen floor. Just high enough to set a bucket under it, he added an elbow and faucet. No more bucketing water across the yard.

I still subscribed to *Arizona Highways* Magazine and held forth on the subject of moving there at every opportunity. Finally Ted said we'd go there if

I could find him a job. I did. Much to his surprise and somewhat to mine. I learned through the Department of Agriculture in Arizona that Harry Hooker of the old Sierra Bonita Ranch near Willcox was looking for a man with Ted's experience. Ted said he'd take it, but reneged when his boss offered him a ten dollar per month raise. I promptly became hysterical, tore up all my *Arizona Highways* Magazines and cried for three days.

Living conditions for the hired help weren't so bad in Arizona, but instead of punching cattle for Hooker as he'd hoped, Ted was put to work in the fields again. He hated irrigating and developed fallen arches from wearing rubber boots every day.

Through the Aggie Agent he finally found another job near Oracle on a ranch belonging to a dentist who raised cattle as a hobby. The dentist was an old curmudgeon, however, and when the opportunity arose to move to the Continental Ranch, we took it.

The Continental, south of Tucson, had just been purchased by the Farmers' Investment Company and Ted was put in charge of the cattle. We lived in a big, airy old house, one of those hip-roofed frame dwellings with a wrap-around porch so popular in early-day Arizona. It was cooled by giant shade trees and heated by a central fireplace. Too good to be true. As was the idea of putting cattle to graze in the desert.

Christmas, 1948   *Alma, Johnny and Ted*   **May, 1955**

[pds: **In 1948, R. Keith Walden relocated his Farmers Investment Company (FICO) from California to Arizona and purchased the Continental Farm to use as his headquarters. After unsuccessful attempts at cattle ranching, then sheep, Keith transitioned his farming operation to pecans in what later became the largest pecan grove in the world.**]

Ted quit when they decided to try sheep and before they got around to selling real estate and planting pecan trees. The dentist at Oracle talked Ted into coming back for a year. Then we moved to Tucson where he developed pneumonia while working in a dairy.

Never mind the house near the dairy where the prevailing wind was off the sewage plant. Or the big house near the city dump which we lived in rent free to keep it from being further vandalized until it was sold. That's the one where we fastened clear plastic over the window frames because all the glass had been broken, where we put the electric fan in front of a tubful of water to cool ourselves in hot weather and dragged the bed in front of the fireplace when it was cold. There was a bathroom, but we had to dip a bucketful of water out of a fifty-gallon drum and fling it down the bowl to flush the toilet. There was a pump and a good well in the yard but the pipeline had been stolen. We filled two buckets at a time and brought them to the house in Johnny's little red wagon.

I tried raising rabbits in the old chicken house but after watching the captivating little creatures grow from pint-size to fryer-size, couldn't bring myself to have them butchered. I tried baby-sitting through an agency, driving to my jobs in our only conveyance, an old Model-T that Ted had found in a salvage yard.

We needed more dependable transportation. The place was too far from civilization to walk. But shopping the used car lots was quite an experience. Ted always asked, "Do you have any really cheap cars?" At the first two lots the really cheap cars didn't look too bad but the batteries were either dead or missing. At the third lot, little Johnny greeted the salesman himself, "Do you have any cars that will start?"

Always friendly, never shy, Johnny was not so helpful at the loan office where we hoped to get a loan on our personal property. The loan office was listing our furniture: Bedroom set, bed and dresser; Breakfast set, table and four chairs; Johnny interrupted politely, "We have boxes to sit on." Fortunately, the man thought that was a joke and we got the loan .

I shall always believe in providence. When we were about to start scraping the bottom of the barrel, Uncle Howard died and his estate was divided among his brothers and sisters. The executor, another uncle and a compassionate man, sent a check for my mother's share to me. We bought a new car and used the rest for a down payment on a new house. I bought a decent outfit and went out and got a decent job. A few months later, after Ted had quit driving a delivery truck for a freight company because of his arthritis, my boss at the air base helped arrange a job for him that he could handle.

Suddenly, with two dependable jobs and a mortgage we could manage, we were back in the real world again. To celebrate, we drove to New York, going by way of Niagara Falls, stopping to visit Raymond and the boys, my mother's sister and my father. We returned by way of Virginia's Skyline Drive decked in brilliant autumn finery.

Even more exciting and the forerunner of many excursions to come, was our Labor Day weekend in San Diego a year later. We visited Marine Land, the Zoo and attended a performance of the city's magnificent bicentennial pageant.

Uncle Howard Willet Henderson, who died on October 12, 1950 at age 63.

[pds: In the spring of 1957, when I was 18 and just out of high school, I could stand it no longer — I just *had* to visit my mother. Since my father divorced her when I was 5, I'd seen her but once, during Mom's 1951 "grand tour" of New York State. (I was 12.)

So I boarded a Greyhound bus and headed for Tucson. I still remember how nervous I was when she picked me up at the bus station. What would she say – or do? Would she reject me?

My fears were unfounded. None of them were true. She loved me and I loved her. Mom took me home and shoehorned me in as part of the family, along with Ted and Johnny. My visit lasted 3 months. (But that's another story.)]

15 – LIFE IS A CAMERA: SMILE PLEASE!

The one imperfection in our San Diego trip was the fact that on the first night we couldn't find a place to stay and had to sleep in the car. We hoped we'd never have to do it again. Hope hardened into determination and resulted in our building rudimentary house on wheels, a plank-sided, canvas-roofed shelter over the bed of our pickup. Ted installed a shelf along one side as a bed for Johnny and built a moveable chuck-wagon-type box which we could shove out on the tailgate. We cooked on a Coleman stove. Ted and I slept on a mattress on the pick-up floor.

Alma Ready: Lookin' good at 52.

After a shake-down cruise on Mt. Lemon, we ventured farther afield on weekends, still farther on holidays and finally spent an unforgettable vacation in Yellowstone Park. Besides exploring most of Arizona's beauty spots and historic sites, within five years we had visited Nevada's Death Valley, Crater Lake, New Mexico's White Sands, the Colorado Rockies, Salt Lake City, and Banff and Glacier National Parks in Canada.

Our long summer excursions became the pivot around which our lives revolved. I carried a camera and made copious notes, typed them and included the story of each trip in an album of pictures. Before we had tired of reliving the past, we were planning an adventure for the following summer. It was an education for Johnny and for us. We not only visited scenic and historic areas, but places like a sawmill, a paper mill, a cheese factory and a fish cannery. Our trips were something Ted and I could talk about without antagonism. One of the few things.

Looking back, I can understand that Ted was ridden by a monstrous inferiority complex and tried to compensate by putting me down. But it wasn't easy to live with. My reaction was to become involved in pursuits of my own. Like photography.

A snapshot taken on one of our earliest trips had been chosen by the camera shop as "Picture of the Week." After it happened for the third time, I became seriously interested in photography, seriously enough to subscribe to *Popular Photography* and to submit entries to every contest I became aware of. Eventually I began to want more control over negatives and prints and started making contact prints in a small printing frame. Later I attended an evening photography class at Tucson High School to learn whether I could function in the dark, then persuaded Ted to convert our hall closet to a workable darkroom. I joined the Tucson Camera Club and became a really serious photographer. My first sale was to *Arizona Highways* **[pds: November 1962 edition]**, the pictures to be used as illustrations for the story of old

Charleston, a story I had written after we spent a weekend camping on the site during the javelina season. My practice of writing up our adventures had started to pay off.

The *Highways* then accepted my story of "Manzanita" **[pds: October 1963]** and its occurrence in Arizona and another pictures-with-text account of the many beautiful grasses to be found in the state **[pds: "down where the**

GRASSES grow", June, 1963]. They commissioned me to do several pieces for a forthcoming issue featuring Santa Cruz County. Meanwhile, I had been doing a series of picture pages for *Arizona Republic*'s Sunday Magazine, *Days and Ways*. I was living in a new and fascinating world.

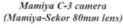
Mamiya C-3 camera
(Mamiya-Sekor 80mm lens)

John had proclaimed his independence by getting a job as a bus boy and at the age of sixteen, borrowing from his boss to buy a car without consulting his parents. On the day after he graduated from high school he rushed off with a buddy for a job at his friend's grandfather's riding stable in Michigan's Upper Peninsula. We were never a family again. Johnny was home briefly before leaving for Korea and later, Vietnam. Soon after he returned from 'Nam, he set up housekeeping with the girl who later became his wife. **[pds: Since Vietnam, John had been treated for exposure to Agent Orange.]**

I had put together a portfolio of pictures of Santa Cruz County which we had explored so thoroughly, and wanted to share them. But I was ahead of the times. The world wasn't yet ready for a black-and-white picture book unless the photographer was an Edward Weston or Ansel Adams. After a long and disheartening effort to find a publisher, I was advised to provide a text, "to tie the pictures together." I envisioned full-page pictures alternating with tidbits culled from the county's history, but when I consulted the librarian in Nogales I discovered the county's history had never been written. I decided to write it.

To do the job right, I needed to live in Santa Cruz County. In May, 1967 I leased an apartment for a year and joined the local historical society. Ted had no objection and for several months he spent one weekend in Nogales and I spent the next in Tucson. But early in the fall he said someone wanted to buy the Tucson house and he suggested we sell it. I helped him find another place to live and we continued our alternating week-end visits. At Christmastime I discovered he had told his foster sisters that I had left him. Our weekends became less frequent.

Desert Tortoise, alias D.T., alias gopherus agassizi was picked up late yesterday, heading north up a wash near Tucson.

the
ARMED FUGITIVE

photographs, Alma Ready

16 – MAKING HISTORY

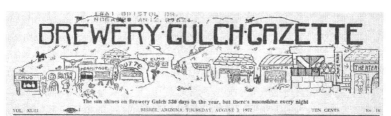

BREWERY GULCH GAZETTE

The sun shines on Brewery Gulch 330 days in the year, but there's moonshine every night

VOL. XLIII   BISBEE, ARIZONA, THURSDAY AUGUST 3, 1972   TEN CENTS   No. 16

THE BREWERY GULCH PHILOSOPHER says –

Ghosts Walk in the Huachucas

By BILL EPLER

Former Langford home with screened transoms still stands at Sunnyside.

Now rusty with disuse, these circular saws were efficient in their day.

Down In Cochise County

By GEORGE BIDEAUX

WEATHER

Soon after I moved to Nogales, the *Arizona Republic*, the state's largest newspaper, was desperately seeking a replacement for their Southern Arizona correspondent, who had left the country. A friend talked me into applying for the job and they hired me. As I said, they were desperate. So desperate that they agreed to teach me how to report the news by phone. I worked for them for two years before I met my editor in person. At the age of sixty I started a new career.

What with all the research and field work necessary – for both jobs – it took me six years to finish the county history. It was well-received and has been reprinted twice. I worked for the newspaper for fourteen years and also did a little freelance writing.

[pds: "Ghosts Walk in the Huachucas" (see previous photo) is an example, from Bisbee, Arizona's *Brewery Gulch Gazette*, dated August 3, 1972. Alma often used husband Ted as a ready-made prop in her photos.]

Alma Ready (l.) with Anne Simpson (Pat's wife) at home in Mariposa Manor (1100 Mariposa Road), Nogales. 1980s.

I have been very happy here. The country is beautiful, the "Border Culture" fascinating, the people friendly and the climate near-perfect. This is where I feel at home.

For two years, Alma did a full-page photo feature each month for the local weekly, *The Nogales International.*

I doubt if Ted would have been happy anywhere. After he had lived in several rented houses in Tucson, I persuaded him to buy a mobile home to be kept at Arivaca Junction, halfway between Tucson and Nogales. There we could meet at the end of each day. He bought the mobile home but kept it in Tucson. After moving it twice he bought another house and I placed the mobile home here in Mariposa Manor **[pds: February, 1974]** where I have lived for nineteen years.

[pds: On Wednesday, March 12, 1986, after a long illness, Ted died at the V.A. Hospital in Tucson, Arizona. Alma scattered his ashes on a Saturday, April 5, and wrote this in her journal:

"Lovely salmon pink sunrise – felt this was the day to scatter Teddy's ashes. Drove, alone, to the San Rafael Valley, via the Harshaw Road turnoff before you reach Harshaw…took road north toward the lone peak. Bright clear sky with a few scattered clouds moving in the breeze. Grassy hills reaching toward distant mountains in four directions. Nothing man-made in sight anywhere except a fence along road. A few cows in distance. Two calves bedded down not far away. Opened the container and walked toward the east with the wind taking the ashes little by little. Was strangely moved – which I hadn't expected. Suddenly felt that Teddy was free at last. And I suddenly realized that an era had ended, finally."]

Those were busy years for me. To keep up with the news I made the rounds of the town every day, attended every city council, county supervisor's and school board meeting, and became very active in the Pimeria Alta Historical Society.

I was also a frequent visitor at the municipal palace in Nogales, Sonora and at the office of the daily paper over there. I spent evenings writing and did all my own photo processing. I often made Saturday trips to Tucson and when Ted became hospitalized, visited him every week. On Sundays there was the hiking club, an informal group that explored the hills and learned a lot about the local flora from Jack Kaiser, botanist and U.S. agricultural inspector at the border.

During the fall and winter months of three different years, along with twenty-five or thirty other earnestly striving adults, I attended weekly evening classes in conversational Spanish – with questionable success.

When Ted and I made our first trip in Mexico we knew no Spanish at all. We had a new car and three weeks leisure time (I had just moved to Nogales), a road map and a certificate showing that the dog had been vaccinated against rabies so we could bring him into the U.S.A. on the way back. We just packed a bag, put the dog in the back seat and took off. We admired the scenery, marveled at the unfamiliar flora and stopped when we got tired. Usually we found someone with a few words of English, If not, we waved our hands around and smiled a lot. We had a wonderful time.

Later I enjoyed trips with the historical society. Two or three times a year they organized a busload or a carload on the train. Ostensibly "historical", the trips tended to be a little touristy, but fun and a real adventure for most of us. They ranged from Cananea and Caborca to El Cañon del Cobre, Guadalajara and Vera Cruz. On our own, a friend and I spent several weekends at Kino Bay.

A few years ago the house next door was bought by a native of Honduras, a delightful middle-aged (young middle-aged) woman who was brought here to be production manager for one of the electronic *maquiladoras* across the line. Lucy is a sharp cookie, likes to wear red and sparkly things, and is a good traveling companion. I enjoy showing her the country I love so well. We've done day trips, weekends and week-long vacations. So far we have covered the highlights of Arizona, Death Valley, the White Sands and the Durango-Silverton train trip in Colorado.

Southern Arizona hiking club, August, 1974. Lee McClure, Alma Ready and James Ross begin their eight-mile trek up Madera Canyon to Josephine Saddle and back.

The Navaho Nation should issue me a permit as a tour guide. I've shown the reservation to my cousin Dottie **[pds: Dorothy Veltman, daughter of Alma's Aunt Alma Veltman]**, my friend Lucy and Johnny's wife, Carole. Pat has asked me to do the same for him and I hope we can do it soon. **[pds: We did! See photos at end of the chapter.]**

After all, it's what the doctor ordered. At my regular check-up in the spring, I was feeling depressed, having just realized that surgery on my spine wasn't the end-all of my problems. That I now have arthritis and will have it for the rest of my life and can't work in the dark room or hike in the hills. And for a year I hadn't *been* anywhere.

Alma Ready and Lucy Hancock - Summer 1987

Last week, when I reported to the doctor again, he said, "You look better. Where have you been?" So I told him about taking Lucy to Salt Lake City. As I left he gave me a four month's supply of my expensive blood pressure pills, saying, "Save your money and take another trip."

I'll be happy to. I've always enjoyed driving and it doesn't tire me. There's nothing I like better than waking up in unfamiliar surroundings. Unless it's just drinking in the beauty of the natural world. If that sounds corny, sorry. But to quote Popeye, "I yam what I yam." I've never been truly appreciative of "art" because to me it's a weak imitation of the real thing. I've loved photography, because to me, it's a reminder of the real thing.

Gradually I've come to accept the fact that I can't get out there anymore and have given my equipment to the high school and my negatives to the historical society. It still bothers me to sit here and see weeds that need pulling and plants that need pruning and not be able to go out there and have at them. Restrained by the doctor's warning and my aching back, I sit here instead and watch the man who does "yard work".

Monument Valley National Park, Arizona
Photo by Patrick Simpson

Arch at Monument Valley, Arizona
Photo by Patrick Simpson

17 – CAT IN MY LAP

Word must have gotten round. Yesterday two small boys, each with a skinny little love-lock hanging below his neck-line, came knocking at my door and asked if I wanted somebody to work in the "jard." Then did I know anybody who need somebody to work in the "jard."

Border area people of Mexican descent whose families evidently speak Spanish at home sometimes pronounce Y like our J. "What do jou want? Why do jou ask?" to me, it's still a little off-putting. And I also wondered what the skinny little kid thought he could do. The handle of my weed-eater would be about level with his nose. But that's life on the border, full of surprises and little mysteries.

My present situation is one of the classic opportunities to "catch up on my reading." I'm one of the library's best customers. And I regularly get a stack of book catalogs as putative head of the historical society's library committee which meets once a month to choose books to be purchased.

As for "creative writing", I've had it. Two years ago, at a friend's suggestion (Why do I listen?), I labored mightily and brought forth *A Very Small Place*, an excellent bibliography of books relative to the history of Santa Cruz County.

So now I lead a quiet life. After years of rushing back and forth scrambling to meet deadlines, hours of yackety-yack, and always having to shape my day to conform with someone else's, it's a pleasure to just sit. To look out the window and watch the birds cavorting in the birdbath or the Johnson grass aimlessly swaying in the breeze, the only sound the distant murmur of traffic on the out-of-sight highway over the hill.

I don't lack for companionship. Catu, my five-year-old feline follows me around all day and keeps my feet warm at night. Big, black and beautiful, he's a watch-cat, a comfort and a clown. He's smarter than I am, doesn't hear me calling unless he happens to feel like it, and makes himself weigh fifty pounds if he doesn't want to be picked up. We play silly games and in the evening, after supper and the TV are over, he sits in my lap and helps me read until bedtime. We're a pretty happy pair.

The End

- No
it
isn't!

Alma's further adventures – and other sequels.

On the road again – Going strong at eighty!

"On my 80th birthday, I decided to visit China. Actually, I had Australia in mind, but for some time I had been looking in vain for a traveling companion.

"Finally, despite horrified shrieks from friends and family, I decided to go alone. I believe that sharing an experience with a friend usually doubles the pleasure, but I also had thought that touring with a group is too regimented. Therefore, being mentally competent (?), in excellent health, and accustomed to fending for myself, I determined to travel solo...."

"Before my plans had jelled, I received a birthday card from my cousin Dottie [pds: Dorothy Veltman]. Ten years younger than I and just returned from two years in Barbados with the Peace Corps, she enclosed a note suggesting a three-week conducted tour of China with a group of senior citizens plus a five-day 'add-on' to Thailand. I said, 'Why not?'"

— (from Alma's unpublished manuscript: *China – Cheers and Otherwise*)

[pds: Why not, indeed? What did age have to do with it, anyhow? When it was all over, Alma wanted to do it again. A year later, she did – this time to South America. Again with Dottie, who brought her friend, Dorothy Johnson. Dottie was 75; Dorothy, 78; and Alma was 82.

From November 10–26, 1989, they took an American Express (El Latino) tour of such places as Machu Picchu in Peru and the spectacular Iguazú waterfalls on the Argentina/Brazil border. After many miles through Ecuador and Chile, encounters with fascinating travelers from around the world, and dozens of hotels, meals and souvenir shops, they returned home – still alive but very tired!

Mom wrote me: "Catu (her cat) was waiting at home. I have done nothing for a week. I may never get on a plane again. Or a bus."]

SEQUEL 1 – MINE, ALL MINE
or
WHY I LIKE THE IDEA OF SELF-PUBLISHING

by Alma Ready

(Appeared in *The Self-Publishing Writer*
Fall-Winter 1975)

A magazine called *The Self-Publishing Writer* had not yet come to my attention in the spring of 1973, but I had just decided to be one.

Naive, uninformed, ignorant, whatever — I had assumed that having finished writing *OPEN RANGE AND HIDDEN SILVER*, a book about a spot on the Mexican border with a unique and exciting history, all I had to do was present it to a publisher and the wheels would begin to turn.

It seemed logical to take it to the University of Arizona Press. There, among other things, my timing was bad. I presented it just before the beginning of summer vacation. The director seemed not too unfavorably impressed — although he did murmur something ominous relative to the use of *old* photographs as "illustrations" — and suggested I leave the manuscript and pictures to await a decision by "the committee." A week later I received a cordial letter acknowledging receipt of the material and also informing me that the committee would not meet again until fall.

I relaxed and enjoyed the summer. Which was just as well. I needed all that stored-up energy when I faced the cold facts in the autumn.

The committee "regretted" by mail. And I never understood just why. I didn't really know the director and didn't have the nerve to ask him. I simply started shopping around for a different publisher. I queried four other western University presses, four independents specializing in western material, and one of the larger houses on the east coast just for the heck of it.

For one reason or another they all "regretted," except one publisher who said he was no longer producing "unsponsored" books and suggested that a book "such as mine" probably could be produced in a limited edition for about $4000. Actually, as I finally have learned, a county history is generally believed to be salable only in the county with which it is concerned. And truthfully, most county histories are pretty sorry affairs

It just happens that the true story of Arizona's Santa Cruz County reads like a sketch for a novel and it would take a pretty lousy writer to obscure the fact. Perhaps the sample chapters I sent out were poorly chosen.

It was my fond hope that the story would sell itself to a book pub lisher, a movie producer* and a producer of a TV series — in that order. I still don't think it was entirely a wild-eyed dream. A friend in New York said he thought there was "a movie in there somewhere." A local historian with a nationwide reputation, in introducing my book to one of his community college classes last winter, asked if I had considered using it as the basis for a novel.

But nothing, absolutely nothing developed and within six months I was devastated. 1 almost put the unpublished manuscript away to be presented to the local historical society after my demise.

Then I learned that Norman Cousins was coming to town. I wouldn't advise anyone else to try it. I couldn't do it again and I very nearly couldn't do it then. But I cornered him. 1 knew he was planning to spend a week at his "ranch" near Patagonia. He had to read something. I thrust the manuscript upon him. The whole thing. "Please," I wailed, "just tell me whether or not I have written a book."

He took it. Probably he was curious about the history of his adopted county. And mine was the first written account. I had done all the research from records, letters, reminiscences, and early newspapers. (I had built a tilt-top table so I could spread out the fragile old sheets, and pored over them night after night for months.)

"The book has very substantial merit and I congratulate you on a professional piece of work," Mr. Cousins said. For me, that settled it. if it was good enough for Norman Cousins it was good enough for me. I would put up the money myself practically my entire life savings and get the thing printed. Trouble was, I didn't know how to go about it.

Back to the U. of A. to my one friend in the publishing business. And a strange sort of friendship it is. We probably wouldn't recognize each other if we met outside his office. Ten years ago when I first got together a batch of photographs I thought would sell, somebody (who?) said "Go see Doug Peck." I wasn't able to market the pictures but Doug liked them. "These aren't just photographs," he said, "they are a way of seeing." I've never forgotten that. I had seen him only once since then but I thought he would remember. And he did.

Doug read the sample chapters and looked over the pictures. He told me to take them to Joe Hulderman's Tucson Typographic Service. Joe is an artist at heart and a superb craftsman. His services are in such demand that he can afford to be discriminating. Luckily for me, he liked my ideas.

Joe also is a man of understanding and infinite patience. He led me through the maze of book production in such a way that everything seemed to happen as a matter of course. We discussed papers and type face and design. He gave me an estimate of $3000 for 1500 copies printed and bound (paper), printing and binding to be subcontracted by his firm. He said 1 could keep costs down by doing my own proofreading and making the index. The deeper I became involved the more I enjoyed it. *OPEN RANGE AND HIDDEN SILVER* was going to be mine, all mine.

Doing the paste-up was time-consuming and frustrating but in the end, the most satisfying job of all. I had definite ideas about how 1 wanted the pictures distributed, placed and sized. I knew how long I wanted the chapters to be and where I wanted them to begin and end. Joe didn't try to change a tiling.

The index was something else. Following the explicit directions in Udia Olsen's *Preparing the Manuscript* made things easier, but I found decisions about what to include and what to leave out extremely difficult to make. Finally even the index was proofed. 1 carried the paste-up and the photo prints to Shandling Lithographic Service and a week or so later Joe and I were invited over to approve the brown line.

The quality of the photo reproductions was disappointing. I had made the prints myself and knew exactly what I wanted. Shandling and Joe convinced me that I was expecting too much of the paper selected and suggested a different grade. It had already become evident that this was not to be a financially rewarding project, largely because 1 was unwilling to go second class in any department. I ordered a more expensive paper.

The design for the cover also was mine and my only disappointment was that the color was not carried over to the spine so the book would be more noticeable on the shelf. We never discussed it and I still don't know if it would have been possible.

The pages were shipped to Roswell Bookbinding in Phoenix and I received my first order from a Scottsdale bookseller before I received the books. Also a very graceful compliment from Mark Roswell, an occurrence which I was told is a rarity. Such things invariably have meant more to me than volume of sales although my saner self tells me that under the circumstances this is ridiculous. I simply cannot afford to *bestow* the book on the reading public. (Another $25 in sales and I will have recovered expenses, including those of the second printing.)

Finally the books arrived and on a beautiful Sunday afternoon in October the manager of the hotel's gift shop and the management of Rio Rico Inn jointly gave a beautiful party in my honor. We sold eighty books, a figure which left them somewhat disappointed but thrilled me to pieces.

The historical society announced the publication, the local radio station (in my debt for past favors) gave it a spot and still repeats it, the local papers (this town of 10,000 runs to one weekly and one "daily" five days a week) carried laudatory reviews. It just happened that within the week a Tucson TV station sent a crew down to cover the 50th anniversary of the Nogales public library. I was invited to participate and the interview was broadcast throughout southern Arizona. The Tucson and Phoenix papers reviewed the book, also the *Journal of Arizona History*, the *Arizona Cattlelog* and *Sunset Magazine*. That was it, but it was free.

The historical society has mentioned my book several times in its regular news letter. GAC Corporation, developers of Rio Rico (where I own a lot) have given me advertising space in two issues of their month news sheet. The only money 1 have spent for advertising was for printing 1000 mailers and sending out three or four hundred of them immediately after the book appeared. The returns were practically nil. I had intended to mail them to other historical societies but was never able to wangle a list of such. I no longer think it would have been a good idea. Local groups seem to be interested in their own little corner of the world and not much else. In my experience, best use of the mailers has been to send them to individuals known to be likely prospects.

The local historical museum is selling my book and so is my hairdresser. The hairdresser sells the most. I persuaded two motels and a drug store in Nogales to take twenty copies each for a one-time introductory run, but they refused to reorder because it was a nuisance. A couple of gift shops down the highway sell a few copies. After a year-long hassle over a couple of debatable dates, the Tumacacori National Monument has decided to handle it. Several stores in Tucson and one in Scottsdale reorder regularly in small quantities.

In Santa Cruz County there is no book store. I know it's hard to believe but until three weeks ago there was no book store south of Tucson. Now there is one store at a retirement community 45 miles north of Nogales. I have made about half my sales to people I have met at the post office, the court house or on the street. Being a news correspondent has made this easier since I am on the street every day. And I haven't been bashful about it.

But I have turned down invitations to speak at various civic club meetings, an attitude I have been told is foolish. But I'm not a good speaker. I'm afraid I would bore people instead of turning them on. Besides, the thought of speaking before an audience scares the hell out of me.

I rationalize it this way. I enjoyed writing the book. I had fun putting it together. Launching it and receiving the good wishes of a lot of fine people gave me a lot of pleasure. Why spoil it by making a "do or die" thing out of selling it? No amount of high pressure salesmanship at this point is going to put the project on a paying basis. Cost of printing and binding was a fraction over $2.00 per copy. The book sells for $5.00. The store get $2.00. Figure it out for yourself.

However, the book is not going to go out of style. It is the only written history of an extremely interesting area and is likely to be the only one for quite a while. Orders probably will continue to trickle in and provide me with pocket money for several years.

At the end of the first year I had disposed of 1200 copies and was persuaded (too easily?) to order a second printing of 1000 at a cost of $1500. I still have a hundred copies of the first edition. In my mobile home there is a nook designed to house a washer and dryer. That second printing, still sealed in dust-proof cartons, fits nicely into the nook. Like I said -pocket money. For my grandchildren?

At present I have no intention of writing another book. I'm still resting. The strain of producing a first book at the age of 66 requires a bit of extra time for recuperation. And a daily stint of making like a correspondent for the Arizona Republic more or less satisfies the urge to write *something.*

But if ever I should write another book I would publish it myself without question. For one thing I would want it done my way. I also would want it done where I could keep an eye on things. Lastly, if by some quirk of fate the income should exceed the cost of production, the profits would be mine alone.

What brought all this about? What was the cause of my writing a book in the first place? A long-standing love affair with this little patch of earth and an insatiable urge to share what I had found with others not lucky enough to have seen it for themselves.

Incidentally, the fact that my feeling for the natural beauty of the land equals my interest its history, probably accounts for the "difference" remarked by several reviewers of my book. Also, although we had been regular visitors to Santa Cruz County for twenty years, our home was in Tucson. As an "outsider" I was able to maintain a detachment impossible to the county historian who so often is a member of a local family.

For several years my husband and I had spent our spare time wandering through these hills and valleys attempting to capture their charm on film. When I had accumulated a sizable folder of photographs 1 called on Doug Peck again, this time for advice about producing a picture book. He suggested using history-oriented captions to tie the pictures together. At Shandling Litho they advised me to drop the whole idea. Picture books in black and white wouldn't sell, they said. But in investigating the possibility, I had discovered that the county history never had been written.

At this point my very old father died, leaving me a few hundred dollars which I felt free to squander. I leased a small apartment in

Nogales and allowed myself a year for research. I proposed to write the history myself.

In less than six months the area correspondent for the Phoenix newspaper moved out of town and I was hired to fill the vacancy. The job gave me a new insight on county life and numerous valuable leads to historical information. Luckily it also paid the rent. At the end of the year I found that work on the history was just beginning. I gave several evenings a week and most weekends to the project for nearly six years. As I resurrected early-day events in the life of the community in chronological sequence I could hardly wait to learn what happened next. After I got it all together I could hardly wait to tell everybody all about it.

If you haven't read *OPEN RANGE AND HIDDEN SILVER*, let me sell you a copy. You'll love it

SEQUEL 2 – A HISTORY OF THE BLACK OAK CEMETERY

by Alma Ready, 1976
(With information supplied by Cora Everhart)

Residents of the Canelo-Elgin-Sonoita area, in Arizona's Santa Cruz County, live there because they like it. Mostly pioneers, or sons or grandsons of pioneers, they love the land, its beauty and comparative peace and quiet, and intend to spend their lives right where they are. When they die, they want to be buried in the Black Oak Cemetery.

Except for a 130,000-acre Mexican Land Grant (1832-Elias) along the little Babocomari River, which was purchased by Dr. E.B. Perrin after the Civil War (having been abandoned to the Apaches in 1849) the area was penetrated by non-Indians quite recently. The northern section was settled almost all at once between 1910 and 1913. The Parker family already was situated south of the pass in Parker Canyon in the 1880's, And a small settlement had developed near the Elgin station after the railroad came through in 1881.

Earlier, however, possibly a dozen families had settled on widely scattered ranches in the general vicinity of Canille (now found on the map as Canelo) where the Elgin-Canille road intersected the road to Ft. Huachuca. The place was sub-irrigated, a garden spot with access to both Ft. Huachuca and Tucson markets, one of the few places in southern Arizona where dry farming could be made profitable.

Early residents were Mrs. Hattie Johnson and her son Jim Finley; "Uncle Billy" Parker and his wife, "Aunt Addie"; Robert A. Rodgers, forest ranger and his family; Mal Eason, a bachelor; William Bowers and family; Mr. and Mrs. John McCarty and sons George, Pat and John; B.K. Wilson and family; Mrs. Laura Parsons and family; and George Beyerly, Star Route mail carrier (Canille to Elgin); and several loners living in mountain cabins including Tom Wills and John Clary.

Canille had a post office established in 1904 and the first school in the east end of the county. Living comparatively lonely lives as individuals, the settlers had a tendency to organize for the purpose of getting together on a regular basis either to socialize or to discuss problems common to the group.

The first Elgin Settlers' Picnic was held in the late summer of 1912 and still is an annual event. The first Santa Cruz County Fair was held at the Sonoita crossroads in 1910. Other organizations in the east end of the county were the Elgin Community Club (still functioning) and the Vaughn Adobe Church, now disbanded, the building reduced to a mound of rubble beside the road.

One of the problems facing every pioneer community was locating and maintaining a place to bury its dead. Until the isolated rangers' apprehension of the last renegade Apache, isolated ranchers had been forced for safety's sake, to dig graves within sight of their homes. Small settlements had placed their cemeteries close to the edge of town. Increasing population and rapid development now was making it necessary in many cases to move the graves and re-bury the bodies. In some instances, old bones simply were tossed away.

The people at Canille wanted a cemetery that would be permanent, a place where eventually they could rest in peace.

Mrs. Hattie Johnson, one of the earliest settlers, who presided over the Canille school board as gracefully as she managed her ranch or galloped after range cattle riding side-saddle across the prairie, picked a site. Having previously lived in Tucson, she now had been ordered to re-bury her dead. She urged the settlers to petition the National Forest Service for permission to use ten acres as a free permanent cemetery.

Their request was granted and on April 1, 1917 a Special Use Permit was issued. Since the Canille School District 10 was the only legal body representing the public in the area, the permit was made out in their name. For safekeeping, the document was given over to the president of the board, Mrs. Johnson, where it remained until her death early in the 1940's. Her family's re-burial was the first in the new burying ground.

Robert A. Rodgers, who also was the postmaster at Canille, was Ranger of the Coronado Forest Canille district at the time. The map which accompanied the permit was made by his son-in-law, Stanley P. Young, Ranger of the Huachuca District, The cemetery, as shown, lies two miles northwest of Canille (now spelled Canelo) and seven miles southwest of Elgin.

Mrs. Johnson and other interested settlers met once a year at the Elgin Club where they paid voluntary dues to the loosely organized Black Oak Cemetery Association, paid bills, and transacted any necessary business connected with the maintenance of the cemetery.

In 1929 the group decided that in order to protect and properly maintain the cemetery, at least five acres should be fenced. They appointed a committee to collect funds for the project and also to petition the county board of supervisors to construct a sixty-foot road leading from the Elgin-Canille road to the cemetery gate.

The supervisors had no objection but informed the committee that one of the legal requirements was to post a notice of intent at each end of the road, at the Elgin post office and at the door of the courthouse in Nogales. The notices were to be posted 30 days before presentation of the petition. By the time A.J. Johnson and Charles Reeves got the posters printed and tacked up on the buildings, time had almost run out. So at 8:00 p.m. on a chilly night in May, they drove out to the cemetery and bumbled around in the dark getting the signs up at each end of the road.

Cora Everhart, Carrie Fraizer and chairman, Mrs. Charles (Lillie) Reeves had collected $126.00 in cash and solicited other contributions.

On the Sunday before Memorial Day Committee "and others" met at the cemetery. Secretary-treasurer Everhart's notes, penciled on yellowed foolscap on May 30, 1921, still exist. They read in part: "Posts have been set, the iron gates placed and most of the woven wire stretched. Last Sunday, while the men and boys cleaned up the grounds and stretched the woven wire, the ladies served a basket lunch."

The secretary noted that the committee wished to express their thanks for (1) some posts, Mrs. W.A. Parker, (2) Notary fee not collected, Mr. Le Gendre, (3) 240 rods of pony wire, Mr. Larrimore, (4) staples, Mr. Ramsey, (5) assistance in stretching the woven wire. And lunch. A list of 33 names of cash contributors follows.

The report also noted expenses of $84.25 for woven wire and gates; $12.00 for post holes and setting of posts; $25.00 for posts.

On Memorial Day, May 30, 1929, the cemetery was dedicated. In Mrs. Everhart's words, "Loyally assisted by members of the Vaughn Adobe Church, Rev. Sleath conducted the open air ceremony in the presence of 200 persons. We listened to a moving sermon. Many were moved to tears. To a portable organ, the crowd sang hymns. One solo, a lady sang in tremolo. In the open on a perfect day, the ceremony was most effective."

The trustees of the Canille school board were instructed by the county supervisors, that after the cemetery was dedicated to the use of the community, they must budget each year for its upkeep.

Affairs of the association proceeded without incident except that in 1931 the board found it necessary to appeal to Ranger O. J. Olson for an opinion regarding designation of lots. In his reply to chairman Mrs. Charles Reeves, Mr. Olson made it clear that designation of lots to individuals was the responsibility of the board.

When the Canille school district was annexed to Sonoita school district #25 in 1950, members of the Sonoita school board automatically became trustees of the cemetery. As the population shifted, the Elgin, Vaughn and Rain Valley school districts also were annexed to Sonoita, and in line with the changes, residents of the other areas inherited cemetery privileges along with the original members of the association.

Over the years, various groups in the area had their special interests but the one common to all was the maintenance and improvement of the Black Oak Cemetery. The Elgin group had been most active in fencing the five acres and obtaining the access road. Also laying out roads and paths within. Mark C. Turney and his wife, Ida, donated the wrought iron entrance gates. Ida assumed the responsibility of notifying the members of the annual meeting each year.

Mattie Johnson's son, James Finley, built an altar in a chapel which Mack Wood helped design. Situated at the east end of the central avenue, it was roofed and floored but open on three sides. He also set up a trust deposit of $10,000. in the Valley National Bank, the income from which is to be used for maintenance. The association built a small store-house and bought chairs for the chapel and power tools for cleanup work.

In the late 'Sixties several problems arose. For one thing, it often proved difficult to locate lots which had been marked earlier without the aid of a surveyor. It was rumored that the forest service was going to "close down" the cemetery. And the group had begun to realize that it was too loosely organized to take effective action in many cases.

A handful of activists decided that something must be done. Just previous to the annual meeting in 1972, a re-survey of the cemetery was made by Robert Lenon. His research turned up a map made by Hugo Miller in 1929 at the time of the construction of the access road. It showed that about 2 1/2 acres of the five acres fenced off was not covered by the permit. The association had not known of the existence of the map.

At the membership meeting on Feb. 13, 1972, the following proposals were brought forward for consideration: (1) Incorporation, (2) Trading 2 1/2 acres unfenced for the 2 1/2 acres enclosed by the fence by mistake, (3) Requesting an outright gift of the 10 acres to the association by the Forest

Service.

Wagner Schorr, Cecil Honnas and Cora Everhart were named as a committee to resolve problems of incorporation with the assistance of attorney L.B. Solsberry. Mrs. Everhart was to contact the Ranger concerning the trade of 2 1/2 acres. The proposal to request the cemetery as a gift was tabled. Officers elected were president, Richard Bunnell, Elgin; secretary-treasurer, Mrs. Lou Schock, Elgin; vice-president, Mrs. Robert Townsend, Rain Valley Ranch, Elgin.

Preparation of articles of incorporation was started immediately and they were filed in Phoenix in April 1972. Incorporators were: Wagner Schorr, Cecil Honnas, and Cora Everhart.

Several months later, Ranger Adrian Hill advised that instead of trading 2 1/2 acres, "location" of the cemetery could easily be corrected simply by correcting the area description in the permit and correcting the map to match. He also said rules and regulations for funerals as per the State Board of Funeral Directors and Embalmers should be part of the by-laws. He went over the proposed by-laws and found some unacceptable and they were changed accordingly. Mr. Hill also showed the committee a copy of a map made in 1941 by Snow and Bentley at the request of the Forest Superintendent for distribution to the school districts involved. This was the first time members of the association had seen it. It showed only 5 acres.

Mr. Hill was succeeded on or about Jan. 1, 1973 by Kenneth Bishop, Ranger of the Huachuca District, who expressed a desire to attend our membership meetings and was invited to do so.

At the first membership meeting of the Black Oak Cemetery Association since incorporation, which was held at the Elgin clubhouse February 11, 1973, the by-laws were adopted. The treasurer's report showed a balance of over $3,000. Up to the present time, donations and grants have more than paid for cemetery expenses and no tax has ever been levied. Stone Collie, Cecil Honnas and Wagner Schorr were elected directors. It was agreed that the annual meeting of members will continue to be on the second Sunday of each February at 2:00 p.m. and that the board of directors will meet immediately afterward.

According to the rules and regulations, burials are free and will be restricted to (1) Pioneer residents of the Sonoita School District and their direct descendants. Pioneers are considered to be those who have resided in the area 20 years prior to December 31, 1973. (2) Those who have been assigned lots prior to January 1, 1973. (3) Those who already have direct descendants buried in the cemetery. (4) Persons who may be approved by the Executive Committee (subject to #3) or who, due to other compelling circumstances should be eligible for approval. No-one is to acquire title to a lot but only the right of burial. There will be no restrictions as to race, color, or creed.

Situated on high ground overlooking the low rolling hills with distant views of the Santa Ritas and the "Biscuit," and with the mass of the nearby Huachucas for a backdrop, the park-like cemetery amid a grove of native evergreen oaks, is a place of natural beauty and serenity. Thanks to the dedication of a few individuals, the place belongs to the area's pioneers and their descendants in perpetuity.

SEQUEL 3 – *LA ARIZONA*, SONORA

by Alma Ready, 1977

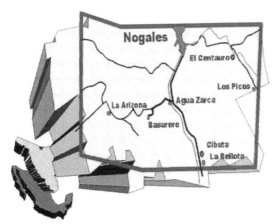

La Arizona is never visited by tourists. The ranch is twenty miles from nowhere, "over the mountain", and reached by one of the roughest roads known to man. It is also several miles south of the international border and about twenty miles west of Nogales in Sonora.

But the story behind this gem enclosed in a matrix of rugged little mountains reads like the outpouring of someone's imagination.

The Papago Indians who called the place *ali shonak* (phoneticized by the Spanish as *Arizonac* or *Arisona*) for the living springs at the head of a stream, apparently had been familiar with the area since time began. When the Jesuit Padre Eusebio Kino began his ministrations in northwestern New Spain in 1687, a handful of the Indians were settled there on a mesa overlooking the valley where flows the rivulet which is one of the main tributaries of the Altar River.

When Kino established a mission headquarters at Saric, ten miles west by an almost impassable trail, Arizonac became a *visita*, a place to which the missionaries made occasional visits.

Saric is remembered for the renegade Luis of Saric who led the Pima uprising in 1791 when one thousand savages in war regalia burned twenty "whites" alive in Luis' house, set fire to the church at Tubutama, murdered the priest at Caborca, forced the residents at San Xavier del Bac to flee and killed more than a hundred persons before retiring to the Santa Catalina Mountains north of Tucson.

The name "Arizona" seems to have appeared in print for the first time when the *Real de Arizona* was established in 1730 by Gabriel Prudhon, Alcalde Mayor of Sonora. A handful of people, lured by traces of precious metals in the hills, had attempted to settle there, despite devastating Apache raids, and six years later their audacity paid off with the discovery of the *Planchas de Plata* or *Bolas de Plata* silver deposit, one of the richest surface discoveries ever made anywhere in the world.

Free silver was found in enormous slabs and balls, one of which is known to have weighed 2700 pounds, and the name, Arizona, reached all of Europe. King Philip V of Spain issued a decree declaring the find a "curiosity" and therefore all his – instead of collecting the usual "royal fifth" – a move which led to considerable bootlegging in silver. Capt, Juan Bautista de Anza, commander of the nearest presidio and father of the Anza who forty years later lead the famous colonizing expedition to San Francisco, was ordered to confiscate the treasure but soon was forced to report that mining had ceased arid tie miners scattered to more lucrative prospects.

The Jesuits were expelled from New Spain in 1767, the little settlement of Arizona was deserted soon after, and because the government was unable to provide military protection, the whole area was in effect, "given back to the Indians."

The *Planchas de Plata* itself was "lost". It was rediscovered soon after the Gadsden Purchase in 1854, by a party of American miners who took out a nineteen-pound chunk of silver before being forced by Sonoran authorities to retreat north of the Mexican border where they relocated the old mines at *Ajo* instead, thereby beginning the first successful mining operation in what was to become Arizona Territory.

Two years previously, in 1852, the Count Raousset-Boulbon had appeared on the scene with a party of two hundred Frenchmen recruited in the San Francisco area among recent immigrants disillusioned with prospects in the California goldfields.

Raousset proposed to make his headquarters at Saric, re-open the *Planchas de Plata* and explore the country for other "desirable lands, mines and placers", all of which were to be shared with a corporation which had been formed in Sonora with government approval.

Soon serious misunderstandings arose. Raousset was .accused of planning to make himself "Sultan of Sonora" and six weeks after reaching Saric ne was ordered to leave the country. He retaliated by leading his company in a march against Hermosillo and for a time, held the city. The pueblos refused to join him in a general revolt however, and in the end the French were forced to return to San Francisco.

Two or three years before Raousset, another young man had arrived in

Hermosillo quite as remarkable, but in a very different sort of way.

William Barnett, who in 1840 with his parents and two brothers had immigrated to Virginia from his birthplace in Cornwall, England, had then moved with the family to San Francisco. His brothers became involved in mining in California but William's interests lay farther south, In Hermosillo he seems to have quickly accumulated a wealth of friends and distinguished himself by marrying the lovely Juanita Sanchez despite the fact that her parents had shipped her off to a convent to prevent her marrying a gringo.

Barnett then proceeded to demonstrate his organizational ability, his powers of persuasion, and his astonishing self-confidence. Not permitted to own property in Mexico because he was a citizen of the United States, Barnett persuaded five friends to file in his stead, homestead claims on five adjoining parcels of land in the *Real de Arizona.*

He moved into his northern stronghold bag, baggage and bride, and to all appearances lived happily ever after. He was not even bothered by the Indians. For the next thirty-five years soldiers of the United States and Mexico chased Apaches up and down canyons and over mountains on both sides of the border less than ten miles from his doorstep, but *La Arizona* was unmolested. Barnett apparently was one of those rare persons who understood how to get along with the natives.

He built a home on the 60,000-acre place, made it self-sustaining, and subsequently increased his holdings considerably, adding among others, the parcel on which the *Planchas de Plata* was located.

When his sons came of age — there were nine — he arranged to have the title to 5,000 hectares (approximately 12,000 acres) turned over to each one, and gave him three hundred cows. He built homes near his own for those who chose to remain on the place after they married.

Incidentally, three of his sons were born of William's second marriage, a circumstance the family tends to overlook since the affair was never sanctioned by the church.

During his lifetime Barnett maintained complete control of the ranch, however. Under his direction cattle roamed the hills, flatlands along the river were cultivated, orchards planted, and a grist mill was operated by waters of an acequia. There was a tannery, and later a small general store for the workers who lived on the ranch. The women on the place were skilled in weaving blankets and in drying fruits and vegetables for winter consumption. The only "essentials" *La Arizona* didn't produce were coffee and tobacco. Hides were sent to market and surplus beef was made into jerky and sold to the Mexican government for use of the navy.

But this was no pioneer-type, log cabin existence. Barnett's house was half the size of a city block, built of adobes around a courtyard, with earthen floors and ceilings finished with native bamboo laid over the beams. The spacious rooms had eighteen-foot ceilings and there was a verandah over-looking the river. A cavernous fireplace stretched across the width of the kitchen where hams and sides of bacon were hung to smoke while meals were cooking, Some of the furnishings were elegant and are now prized possessions of William's descendants.

Barnett died in 1909 at the age of seventy-nine and one of his grandsons has the papers to prove it. At least he has a copy of the death certificate which so states. Also papers attesting to the fact that William and his two brothers had immigrated to Virginia with their parents in 1840.

If William was seventy-nine in 1909 it works out that at the time of his removal to *La Arizona* from Hermosillo, he was nineteen years old, quite young to have acquired a wife and already have made a name for himself. That William did, in fact, take over *La Arizona* in 1849 is attested by documents in the possession of a Nogales, Sonora businessman who is one of William's great-grandsons on the maternal side of the family.

Perhaps in later years, William allowed his family and friends to think he was younger than he actually was. Persons of such exceptional vitality often appear younger than their contemporaries and sometimes like to preserve the illusion. A little hanky-panky certainly seems to be indicated somewhere along the line. A copy of an affidavit dated 1908 is extant wherein William asserts that he is a citizen of the United States and claims to have been born in the State of Illinois, another statement that doesn't appear to square with the facts.

Who knows now, which dates are correct and why William was so determined to maintain his United States citizenship? Presumably his children were citizens of Mexico by virtue of having been born there.

At any rate, after Barnett's death the home place was sold by his heirs to the West Coast Cattle Company of Tucson, an outfit which later borrowed a large sum of money from Joe Wise of Nogales, Arizona.

Joe, son of Morgan R. Wise, former U.S. Congressman from Pennsylvania, who had homesteaded at Calabasas (near Nogales) in 1886, was postmaster at Calabasas for twenty years and later served a term as mayor of Nogales. He had many business interests. When the cattle company defaulted on the loan in 1919, Joe took over *La Arizona* and hired a manager to run cattle on the place. Ten years later when his son, Joseph Knight Wise, became partner in the venture, Knight not only managed the business, he made his home on the ranch and became so "Mexicanized" that his two children spoke Spanish only, until they were old enough to be sent to school in the United States.

Knight Wise retained his interest in the ranch when the other heirs disposed of their share of the property after his father's death, and Knight's son, "Pepe", now runs the place and makes his home there.

It was Pepe who drove the jeep, which skidded a little on the icy road approaching the top of the pass. The passengers ducked their heads and clung to the seats trying to ignore the sheer drop at the edge of the narrow mountain track.

Descending to the flat on the sunny side of the mountain, where the rocky cliffs were dotted with organ pipe cactus and an occasional saguaro, the jeep was momentarily halted by passage of a tribe of *chulas*, (coati mundi) those astonishing creatures resembling a cross between an anteater, a raccoon and a monkey. Pepe said they live in small caves pitting the face of a nearby cliff.

Two miles before the road reached the ranch house it skirted a communal settlement (*el ejido*) where about sixty families of small farmers live.

Pepe called them agrarians. He said they first squatted on the land adjoining *La Arizona* in 1953 and the move was legalized ten years later. The government also gave them plots of land along the river, reducing the area of La Arizona by 3,000 to about 12,000 acres.

Much to Pepe's distress, one old man raises goats which respect no property lines. Three or four of the families seem to be knowledgeable farmers. They get their planting done on time and usually make some sort of a crop. "How the rest of them manage to live, I don't know," Pepe said. "They are friendly enough. They spend a lot of time riding up and down the road in beat-up old trucks. But heaven knows where they get the money for groceries."

The elementary school in the village was built many years ago by Joe Wise to replace the little adobe on *La Arizona* which the Barnett boys had attended. The outdoor basketball court with the bright orange backboards was contributed recently by the Mexican government.

The old Barnett place is a crumbling ruin. A fine big house Knight built across the river in the Forties is also being allowed to fall apart because Pepe and his wife were plagued by water standing on the floors after every heavy rain. He is building another house on higher ground. The ancient corrals and barn and blacksmith shop look as they must have looked a century ago.

Pottery shards on a little mesa just across the road from the ranch headquarters indicate that it was once the site of an. Indian village. The chapel for the *visita* of *La Arizona* in Kino's time probably was located here also. Until quite recently the place served as a *campo santo* or cemetery for the Mexicans.

Beyond the *campo santo*, flying enthusiast Knight Wise had cleared a small landing strip within easy walking distance of his own front door. Pepe had no use for it. After an unidentified plane started making frequent and unexplained landings there recently, he decided to give the pilot a rough time. He plowed up the strip.

Two miles up the road are the little man-made twin lakes, a haven for ducks just below "the place where the river is born." This cienaga among the cottonwoods, these rivulets green with cress even though the trees were bare, these sky-reflecting pools with water quietly welling up from unknown depths, the "little springs" were the Papago's *ali shonak*.

This is the place that gave its name to a district known to miners on two continents, later to Arizona City (afterward called Yuma) and still later to the 48th of the United States.

A petition to Congress in 1856 for organization of a Territorial Government for the area between the Rio Grande and the Colorado – the third of fifteen such petitions drawn up before the deed was finally accomplished – included the proposal to name the new Territory "Arizona."

Before President Abraham Lincoln signed the statute creating the Territory of Arizona in 1863, the names Mesilla, Arizuma, Pimeria and Gadsonia had been considered and discarded in favor of the euphonious derivative of the ancient Indian name.

The late historian, Roscoe Willson, after a visit to the place fifteen years ago, suggested an arrangement with Mexico and the State of Sonora whereby La Arizona could he acquired "by the United States and officially designated "Arizona's Birthplace Park."

MAJOR SOURCES

Roca, Paul M. Paths of the Padres Through Sonora, Tucson: Arizona Pioneers' Historical Society, 1967.

Wyllys, Rufus L. The French in Sonora, Berkeley: U. of Cal. Press, 1932.

Documents in possession of William Barnett's grandson, Jerry Barnett:

Nogales, Arizona.

Documents in possession of William Barnett's great-grandson, Eduardo
Robinson: Nogales, Sonora.

Scrapbook of Marguerite Macdonald, daughter of Joseph Wise, Nogales, AZ

SEQUEL 4 – TRINCHERAS

by Alma Ready, 1977

(Appeared in *Nogales International* June 25, 1977)

We were not even sure we had the right mountain. Just a sprawling hunk of brown-black jagged volcanic rock rising abruptly from the desert floor and hacked off at about 900 feet, in northern Sonora, Mexico.

But when we approached close enough to distinguish the carefully constructed stone revetments stretching horizontally across the gently sloping north face, imagination ran riot.

Aerial view of the north side of El Cerro de Trincheras (the Hill of Trenches) taken in 1996 from an ultralight aircraft, including terraces and other architectural elements. In the foreground is the modern village of Trincheras. Photo: Adriel Heisey.

We pictured hundreds of small brown people going about their daily tasks in their terraced courtyards. We imagined them descending and climbing back up the winding trails from the flatland, wearing brimming water jars like crowns.

Why, several generations "before history," an entire people chose to build their homes on 18 or 20 narrow shelves starting a few hundred feet above the

103

plain and rising to the craggy summit, is a matter of conjecture.

Did they undertake the back-breaking labor of building here because they were afraid? The Spanish "trincheras" (intrenchments) suggest that they chose the site for protection. Certainly it would be difficult for an enemy to take the town.

Who were their enemies? Were the Trincheras people overcome? Or did they eventually triumph and move to a spot where life was easier?

If so, they must have missed the spectacular view of Altar Valley. Maybe they just liked it up on the mountain.

Natural erosion and the hoofs of browsing animals have disarranged the rocks shoring up some of the lower terraces, but hundreds of the retaining walls appear to be intact.

Four or five feet high, the mortarless walls reach horizontally for more than 2000 feet in places. In others, the terraces seem long enough for only two or three homes. The flat area enclosed usually reaches back only 12 or 15 feet.

Of the houses themselves, no trace remains. But many stone implements, arrowheads, shell beads and shards of reddish pottery with decorations of a distinctive purplish color have been found.

The northernmost traces of these people were discovered three years ago just north of Nogales, Arizona by archaeologists of the University of Arizona making a pre-construction survey of the Interstate 19 Freeway.

The Nogales site, now obliterated, though evidently once occupied by the "purple pottery people" was not terraced. According to field archaeologist, Quinn Vivian, remains of several huts were found, built half underground and apparently once roofed over with sticks and brush.

Authorities agree that while trincheras are not uncommon in northern Sonora, nowhere do they compare in magnitude to those seen near the village appropriately named Trincheras which we now approached.

A graded road to the dusty little town leads from Santa Ana, 35 miles northeast on Mexico 15. We had not taken that route, however. Since we were on our way to Caborca, it seemed logical to take a cut-across from the Santa Ana -Caborca highway, straight south to the village.

Like many of our "logical" enterprises, it proved somewhat less than practical. The graded road was fine for three miles. For the next seventeen, stretches of powdery sand alternated with areas where naked rocks poked up through the hardpan.

We had dipped and twisted through a forest of palo verde, ocotillo, and bearded cactus, then crossed bleak stretches of wind-scoured plains sparsely covered with creosote bush.

Emerging from a dense thicket bordering a wide dry river we were suddenly confronted by the black mountain, "el cerro", standing guard over a toy-like village of white-washed adobe blocks glaring in the afternoon sun.

At the Ben Hur cantina on the dusty main street, the bartender who spoke no English, summoned the proprietor who also spoke no English but knew some-one who did.

He conducted us to the house of the English-speaking señora, to whom we explained that we would like to take pictures of the mountain, after which we would very much like to have something to eat.

Our new friend made arrangements at el restaurante, then led us by a winding track, to the foot of el cerro. We packed our way a few hundred yards up the rocky slope, took our pictures and retraced our route to el restaurante.

There was one oil-cloth-covered table. Occupied. The young man drinking coffee waved us to a seat. The proprietress appeared from behind a cloth-curtained doorway, smiled and retired.

She soon re-appeared with a plate of goat stew and sliced fresh tomatoes. She brought coffee and round pan and paper napkins. Extra silverware stood in an empty tomato can. Our hostess smiled and retired again.

A round-eyed toddler slowly circled the table while we ate. Two young boys quietly entered and seated themselves in a corner, smiling gently when we glanced in their direction. The young man, whose table we shared, smiled and drank his coffee. Finally, he rose and started for the door. When he reached it, he turned and very carefully said "goodbye".

Through the parted curtain we could see la señora stirring something on a wood-burning cook-stove in the dirt-floored kitchen.

In the dining room, there was a side table on which lay a carton of eggs, some onions and oranges, and a flit gun. In one corner was a glass-fronted kitchen cabinet which housed a set of china dishes.

The two boys still watched us from their crate seats in the other corner.

The single electric light bulb that hung over our table was suspended from a ceiling made of ocotillo wands. Through the screen door, a gentle scattering of powdery sand entered on fitful gusts of warm wind.

When we had finished, we called la señora and asked for la cuenta. "Dos dollas," she said.

"Twenty-five pesos plus tip," we mumbled, calculating. We couldn't remember how to say "thirty" in Spanish.

La señora must have heard the word "pesos." She looked very stern. "Dollas," she said again, holding up two fingers. "Dos dollas."

We stowed away our Mexican money and fished out some United States currency. We gave her two dollars and fifty cents. "OK?" we asked.

"OK," she said, smiling once more.

La señora and the children stood at the open door to bid us farewell.

"Buenas tardes," we said. We turned our back on Las Trincheras and started across the desert toward the highway to Caborca.

SEQUEL 5 – AVIATION IN SANTA CRUZ COUNTY

by Alma Ready, 1979

(Clockwise): 1. Didier Masson was a famous French Aviator, who had been on a barnstorming tour of the United States since 1910. 2. The Sonora ready to take off for a bombing in Guaymas. (Didier Masson is on the right.) 3. Masson's Curtiss Flyer Biplane in flight.

A faded photograph **[pds: not available]** of a hot-air balloon being prepared to ascend from the center of town in old Nogales apparently is the earliest indication of an interest in aviation among residents of the "line City." The picture is labeled "Balloon flight in Nogales during a political rally in the

1800's." No-one seems to know anything else about it, except that it was a hot air balloon filled by building a fire under it.

During the Mexican revolution a few years later, however, Didier Masson, "The birdman who hopes to bomb the Federalist (Mexican) fleet at Guaymas," managed to get not only a picture of his bi-plane but his name and his story in the paper frequently.

The weekly Border Vidette (Nogales) of June 7, 1913 carried a story about Masson's efforts to reach an altitude of 3500 feet necessary to carry out his mission. "He made several practice flights and suffered two accidents but so far he has managed to reach only 1500 feet."

Eventually he made it. For several weeks he bombed the fleet daily, each time dropping two bombs by hand from the open cockpit. He never made a hit.

The public by this time accepted flying enthusiastically as a form of entertainment. "Aeroplane exhibitions by birdmen from Los Angeles" were among attractions promised visitors to Nogales' big two-day 4th of July celebration in 1915.

Shortly afterward, boys who had been playing with firecrackers suddenly became men with guns on their shoulders and marched off to war.

SEQUEL 6 – NOGALES

by Alma Ready, 1984
(Intended for *Voices of the Pimeria Alta* but not used by mistake)

Between Nogales, Arizona and Nogales, Sonora there is a "see-through" fence with a gate, not a wall. Hundreds cross the international line every day to work, to attend church, for entertainment, or to shop. The south side of the line has an especial appeal for tourists. Shops on Obregon and Elias are bursting with hand-blown glass, bright serapes and gay paper flowers. There is music and dancing and the tantalizing odor of Mexican food.

But the tourist who regards Nogales, Arizona as merely the Gateway to Mexico is missing mucho. He who veers away from the main streets long enough to do a little exploring may be happily surprised. Some of the side streets climb to entrancing views of the surrounding countryside. Others, winding up the little side canyons in what could be called "old town" reveal neighborhoods of charming small homes in an infinite variety of architectural styles.

Knowing a bit about the historical background makes any tour more fun. For example, the little hip-roofed adobe three steps below street level at 318 Crawford Street was once the legal residence of Jesse Grant, son of President Ulysses S. Grant. The house on the northeast corner- of Crawford and Sonoita belonged to prominent businessman Bracey Curtis at the turn of the century and served as a home for an influential group of his bachelor friends who called themselves The American Club.

Nogales was not a planned community. It sprang up in the wilderness almost overnight when railways from Kansas City, Missouri and Guaymas, Sonora met at the international boundary on a vast Mexican land grant called Los Nogales de Elias (The Walnut Trees). When the "wedding of the rails" took place on October 25, 1882, a silver spike was driven home by Mrs. William Raymond Morley in bustle and bonnet, wife of the Santa Fe railroad's chief engineer for whom Morley Avenue is named.

Among the spectators was the itinerant merchant, Jacob Isaacson, who was one of the first to recognize the economic potential of the site on the only viable route connecting the United States and western Mexico. He said he had been there a long time, alone except for distant Indian smoke signals and the howling of coyotes. By the time the railroad was completed, a post office called Isaacson had been opened in the trading post established by Jacob and his brother Isaac with Jacob as postmaster. Thirteen months later he had departed and by petition of the settlement's residents, the place was again called Nogales.

On the Sonoran side of the line Juan Jose Vasquez had built a roadhouse and the Mexicans had put up a customs house.

The opening of the railroad triggered a burst of economic activity, most of it centered around mining. Mineralized areas in northern Sonora and southern Arizona were ripe for development, and money lenders all over the world were happy to back up the developers.

Silver was King and returns were largely used to extend operations Cattlemen enjoyed an expanded market, international trade mushroomed, and the service industries in the twin cities multiplied as they thrived.

The town's early growth was haphazard and largely undocumented. What little we know of the first decade comes from a few personal accounts. Lieutenant John Bigelow, Jr., stationed at Lochiel during the last Geronimo campaign in 1886, occasionally traveled to Nogales where he stayed at the Nelson House, a flimsy structure on Nelson Avenue. He reported one other hotel and a third under construction, with "considerable" building going on. He mentioned Brickwood's liquor store with its famous cigar-dispensing booth which straddled the international line in the interest of outwitting the customs collector.

Other establishments began to crowd the line until in 1898 a sixty-foot-wide strip on each side of the boundary was cleared by congressional order at the request of the Customs Service.

Ada EKey Jones, who arrived with her parents in the early 1880a and whose personal efforts to preserve the history of the area have been invaluable, recalled the Proto Brothers' store on Morley Avenue. The eight-by-ten adobe, she said, crowded with sacks of flour and beans and green coffee, projected into the street as did several other buildings, a circumstance which caused considerable difficulty for the city fathers later when they attempted to align the streets to conform to the official Bradford map of 1899.

Six years previously (1893), the town had become incorporated. A town council had been appointed consisting of Theodor Gebler, James B. Mix, Anton Proto, George B. Marsh, and E. B. Hogan. They elected Mix as mayor.

Numerous business houses and many comfortable homes had been built on lots which had been staked out, sold, and re-sold while, according to the Camou-Elias family of Sonora, the area was still part of the Mexican land grant and Nogales residents were squatters.

The council's strategy was to hire the bilingual Henry O. Flipper, first black graduate of West Point and formerly an officer of the U. S. Tenth Cavalry, who was an expert on Mexican land law. Through his efforts the Camou-Elias claim was declared invalid in the United States and the title to the land was cleared. In 1898 Nogales' patent to one square mile of land was signed by President McKinley and deeds to the lots were distributed by Mayor W. F. Overton.

Flipper had surveyed the perimeter. In 1899 engineer William Bradford, "on loan" to the town by the Southern Pacific Company which had acquired the New Mexico and Arizona railroad from the Santa Fe, surveyed the town and prepared the map on which all subsequent property titles have been based.

Nogales had come a long way since Isaacson had put up his little store beside the railroad right-of-way in the pass. There were three or four hotels, one of which, called the Montezuma, was a first-class establishment owned by George Christ, Collector of Customs. Christ, who made his office in the hotel, had persuaded U. S. Customs officials to divide the El Paso District and make Nogales principal port-of-entry for the new Arizona District.

Two influential weekly newspapers, the *Oasis* and the *Border Vidette*, had been established. There were three churches, a public school, and the Territory's largest (20-room) sanitarium. Beside the usual saloons, livery stable and blacksmith shop, assay offices and hardware stores (windmills a specialty), the area supported a foundry, the only cigar factory in Arizona, and a roundhouse and machine shop which serviced the two very profitable railroads. There were several substantial mercantile establishments, two of which, La Ville and Escalada's, were still operative in the 1980s. Two dentists and several doctors were in residence. The town boasted a hank, a first-rate volunteer fire company, an electric light and ice plant, a water company and a local telephone system. In addition, the first Masonic Temple in the Territory had just been built on Terrace Avenue, a dramatic club and an athletic dub hail been formed by the young people of the town, and the Southern Pacific had provided space for a town park on Morley Avenue.

And so in 1897, with a population of 2,000, *mas o menos*, on each side of the line, officials of the twin cities surveyed the situation and believed it was worth talking about. Simultaneously, the Mexicans published a handsome, well-illustrated volume called *El Estado de Sonora, Mexico*, and the Americans in association with the City of Tucson, published *Treasureland*, an informative little book. Both publications give considerable space to the twin cities.

For two decades the city fathers continued to polish their little jewel in its wilderness setting. In 1911 they approved a $170,000 bond issue to put a well on the Santa Cruz at the foot of Proto Canyon and connect it to a reservoir on Court House Hill. In 1918 they covered the open arroyo on Grand Avenue from Crawford Street to Elm.

"The most auspicious event in the history of the Line City" occurred on February 15, 1915 when the whole town turned out for the dedication of the Town Hall, newly erected by the Nogales Volunteer Fire Department. Six years later the city acquired title to the building in exchange for assuming the mortgage.

When the population reached 3,000 in 1919, Nogales was officially proclaimed a city. (Nogales, Sonora had become a city in 1907.) Henceforth, the mayor would he elected by the voters instead of by the council.

The new status was brought to the public's attention by the *Nogales Daily Herald*, established in 1914 and acquired in 1918 by Hansen Ray Sisk who was to continue as editor-publisher until his death in 1969. The paper was still being published in the 1980s by Sisk's wile and son. Its only rival, the weekly *Nogales International*, which had been launched by Craig Pottinger, Sr. in 1925, also continued to appear but had changed hands several times since illness forced Pottinger to sell in 1971.

Though separate, affairs of the two cities continued to be closely linked.- Several Americans had established businesses on the Mexican side and the converse was true. Firefighters from both sides of the line answered alarms from either- side. When in the early 1900s a U.S. military post was established on the outskirts of Nogales, it was not in expectation of trouble between the two countries but to protect U.S. citizens in the event of an accidental spillover of the burgeoning unrest in Mexico.

Two or three "accidents" did occur and the military force at Camp Stephen D. Little had been enlarged to a peak strength of 12,000 by the beginning of World War I. But strict neutrality was observed during Mexico's revolutionary upheavals, and the residents of Ambos Nogales maintained their firm friendship.

Among others stationed here at various times were detachments of the 12th Infantry (white), the 35th Infantry (white), the 10th Cavalry (the famous

Buffalo Soldiers, black), and the 25th Infantry (black). Children of the black regiments were transported to the Frank Reed "school for colored" by a mule-drawn bus.

Camp Little soon became an intrinsic part of life in Nogales both socially and economically. Parades and military hand concerts enlivened holidays and summer evenings. Officers were entertained in private homes and reciprocated by inviting their hosts to military balls and "demonstrations" on the parade grounds. The camp soon spread onto "Cavalry Hill" (Sierra Avenue) and beyond. "Officers' Row" was established on what was later known as Anza Drive. Stables were strung along Ephraim Canyon (Western Avenue) and the base hospital was on the hill at the junction of McNab and Crawford Streets. In 1917 the monthly military payroll was $380,000 and furnishing food and supplies for the camp was a major source of income for many local merchants.

The brilliant young attorney, Duane Bird, son of Allen T. Bird who had edited and published the *Oasis* from 1891 to 1920, was elected mayor in 1921 and a slate of "young Democrats" was elected to the council. They framed a charter for the city (adopted in 1926) which gave the city a maximum of independence from the state.

The Southern Pacific had completed a direct line from Tucson to Nogales in 1910, and in 1927 the line from Nogales to Mexico City became operational making it no longer necessary to travel to the capital city via El Paso. The Nogales International Airport was dedicated in 1928. Momentarily, the future looked rosy.

Then came the "Six Weeks Revolution" in Mexico, several disastrous local floods, and the Great Depression of the 1930s. International trade and travel were disrupted. Banks closed. Camp Little was deactivated. City employees took a fifteen percent wage cut. Many businesses failed.

Work Projects Administration (WPA) funding saved the city from total collapse. Money was allocated for improvements to the pumping plant and the airport, for straightening the Patagonia Road, for lining the arroyo from Walnut Street to Bank's bridge, and to build the Civic Building; also for a stadium and gymnasium at the high school (built in 1916), to lay out Memorial Park, and for a 100-acre golf course and clubhouse on Western Avenue. In 1933 the International Boundary and Water Commission started work on the flood conduit underlying Ambos Nogales.

The World War II years also were difficult for the twin cities. The United States declared war on Japan in 1941 and Mexico immediately followed suit.

Trade was drastically reduced. There was little local industry. Retail merchants were hamstrung by shortages and government rationing of numerous commodities.

Fortunately, many vacationists, prevented from visiting Europe, were discovering America, and one of the places they discovered was southern Arizona. The first "modern" motel was constructed, a resort hotel was extensively remodeled, and Nogales began to call itself Convention City. In 1911 the first Fiesta de los Flores was conceived by some of the towns' enterprising young men as an antidote to depression. The colorful international parade and fiesta with its two "Queens" and spectacular ball was to become an eagerly awaited annual event for the next thirty years.

On August 17, 1945, three days after President Truman announced that war had ended, Ambos Nogales turned out for a giant Peace Parade. A surge of prosperity followed. Trade and tourism kept pace as highway paving was extended to Hermosillo and then to Guaymas. A third customs gate was opened on the international line, solely to handle truck traffic which had begun to rival the railroad. In 1952 designation of Nogales, Sonora as a free port stimulated local retail sales. Movie makers discovered the area and several "big" pictures were filmed in the nearby hills.

A one percent city sales tax was adopted in 1959 and soon afterward an ambitious street paving program was undertaken. The city's first public swimming pool was built at Memorial Park and the Nogales Public Library, organized in 1925, moved into a home of its own designed by award-winning Phoenix architect, Bennie Gonzales. The "new" St. Joseph's Hospital was built on the site of the former golf course.

Mexico's gigantic border improvement program changed the face of Nogales, Sonora in the mid-1960s. A nine-lane U.S. Customs gate on Grand Avenue was dedicated in 1964. Partial completion of U.S. Highway 1-19 spurred local development including construction of the *Parque Industrial* across the line and corresponding plants on this side—the Twin Plant concept. Nogales' economic growth in 1968 was the greatest of any city in the state.

A waste water treatment plant, a joint venture of the twin cities and the International Boundary and Water Commission, was dedicated in 1972. Bypass routes designed to relieve traffic congestion in both cities, met at the border a mile west of Grand Avenue. Mexican and U.S. Customs offices and a truck inspection compound on the American side became operational in 1976. In 1980 products assembled in Mexico under the Twin Plant concept, and Mexican vegetable produce were the major items imported. Nogales ranked as the largest port of entry for winter- vegetables in the world.

Another phase of the city's continual quest for an adequate water supply was construction of a fourth reservoir in 1977 and purchase of the Potrero Water Company the following year. Also in 1978 construction of the city complex on N. Grand Avenue was completed and the municipal government including police and fire departments moved into the handsome new quarters. Subsequently the old Town Hall was used by the Pimeria Alta Historical Society as a museum and archives.

The Nogales High School had held its first commencement exercises in Marsh's Opera House in May 1899. Three young men and two young ladies received diplomas. "High School" at the time, however, was merely space in the crowded elementary school. It was not until 1915 that the high school on Plum Street was built. In 1970 when the Wade Carpenter Junior High School was constructed, four elementary schools were in operation. School Superintendent A.J. Mitchell had put an end to segregation in 1952 simply by announcing that the Frank Reed school was closed. The high school moved into a modern complex of eleven buildings on an extensive campus at the junction of Highway 1-19 and Mariposa Road in 1980.

The First Baptist Church had moved to an adjoining site a few years earlier and the United Churches Fellowship was planning to follow suit. St. Andrews Episcopal had built a facility on Country Club Road in 1968 when the little stone church on Crawford was torn down in the path of the freeway. Sacred Heart on its hill still dominated the center- of town, however-, and several smaller churches maintained their original sites.

Earlier, the lives of two clergymen had become inextricably interwoven in the social fabric of Nogales. One was the Right Reverend Monsignor Louis Duval, pastor of Sacred Heart for nearly forty years beginning in 1905, who enlarged the Catholic church to twice its size, established the parochial school, and promoted the founding of St. Joseph's Hospital. The other was Dr. O.A. Smith, who arrived in 1920 and not only served as pastor of the combined Congregationalist and Methodist churches but was chairman of the Santa Cruz County Welfare Hoard during the Depression, a director of the Chamber of Commerce, and a member of the city board of aldermen for two terms.

Population of Nogales, Sonora in 1980 was estimated at 150,000, a situation favorable to retail business on both sides of the line but particularly troubling to municipal authorities of Nogales, Sonora, who must cope with an influx of newcomers with inadequate housing and an insufficient water supply. U.S. Immigration authorities also felt the pressure of hundreds of aliens who, when the Sonoran city proved to be less than the paradise they had envisioned, attempted to cross the line, documents or no.

Annexation of parcels north and east of the city's original perimeter had brought the area of Nogales, Arizona to twenty square miles and the population to 15,000 in 1980. The increase in revenues resulting from the greater tax base was balanced by the cost of the necessarily larger number of administrative and service personnel, as had been expected. There were minor difficulties, of course, and one serious problem: extensive property damage occasioned by ill-advised construction of homes in the several flood plains. The need for still another elementary school became apparent.

Attractive and substantial homes continued to spring up on the city's outskirts in the early 1980s. At the same time, area residents were becoming increasingly aware of their rich historical background. The Courthouse and Old City Hall had been placed on the National Register of Historic Places, and the possibility of having several neighborhoods designated Historic Districts was under discussion. If a smoke cloud was seen in the 1980s, it probably was a fire department drill. To hear a coyote, it was necessary to camp out in the hills. Jacob Isaacson might had found it an interesting place to visit, but he would not have felt at home in the Canyon de Los Nogales.

SEQUEL 7 – GRINGO RANCHER: WILLIAM BARNETT OF LA ARIZONA, SONORA

by Alma Ready, with Alberto Suarez Barnett

The Journal of Arizona History © 1986 Arizona Historical Society

* * *

A native of New Jersey, Alma Ready is Head of Research at the Pimeria Aha Historical Society Museum in Nogales. A photographer and former correspondent for the *Arizona Republic*, she has written numerous articles about southern Arizona for magazines and newspapers and is author of *Open Range and Hidden Silver*, a narrative history of Santa Cruz County.

The great grandson of William Barnett and a graduate of the University of Sonora, Alberto Suarez Barnett is the founder of the Sonoran Historical Society in Nogales. Sonora. He has worked extensively to promote cultural programs on both sides of the border and is a member of the Board of Directors of the Pimeria Aha Historical Society.

* * *

WLLIAM BARNETT WAS A DARING YOUNG GRINGO who eloped with a beautiful Mexican girl in the early 1860s and, thanks to his own enterprise and to powerful friends in Mexico, created a great mountain enterprise called La Arizona Ranch out of more than 100,000 acres of Sonoran wilderness. It was just below the United States-Mexico boundary and the headquarters was only twenty-five miles southwest of Nogales, but the country was still virgin when Barnett began to develop his holdings in 1870. They included a historic spot, the *Real de Arizonac*, and also the fabulous Planchas de Plata silver deposit, where one of the world's richest surface discoveries attracted scores of miners in 1736. The living spring which gave the *Real*—and later the State of Arizona—a name is located on La Arizona Ranch.

Barnett was in many ways a typical Mexican *hacendado*, ruling a family of nine sons and two daughters with a firm hand and controlling for thirty years the greatest hacienda in northern Sonora. He did this, miraculously, without ever becoming Mexican citizen. His story has never been put together and can be reconstructed only with some difficulty now, but what is known is of extraordinary interest.

The only photograph we have, taken in William's old age, shows him as a still vigorous patriarch. In his younger days, he is said to have made a handsome appearance. Six feet tall, he was a slender, gray-eyed blond with a wide forehead, patrician nose, prominent cheek bones and a tapering, firm chin. Temperamentally he was a romantic adventurer, a man of courage and determination. At the same time he was a resourceful and imaginative businessman, a man of honor and dependability, a father who was dictatorial yet generous. This much we know, that woven into the fabric of his story is a thread of mystery. William himself gave conflicting accounts of his age and his place of birth.

If we are to believe the story he gave to his sons, he was born in the County of Cornwall. England, and at a very early taken by his parents, with his two older brothers, to South Africa, South America, Australia, and finally to Virginia in the States, where his father established an inter-city transportation business. In 1849 the family moved to California, he said, but because of friction among the brothers, he left home, cutting all family ties irrevocably.[1]

William told more than one story. Information placed on his family's birth certificates was certainly less consistent. On his daughter Carmen's in 1888 he gave his age as fifty-seven, which would make his birth year 1831. On the certificate of his granddaughter Leonor in 1899,[2] his age was listed as seventy, which would put his birth date in 1829.[3] In an application for a passport which he presented to the U.S. consul in Nogales in 1908, he stated that he was born on December 18, 1829.[4]

William was no more consistent in identifying his birthplace. On different birth certificates he claimed Chicago, St. Louis, and Pontoosuc, Illinois. Was he an Englishman, or wasn't he? The odds are, he was.

One part of his story can be tentatively verified. His grandson Jerry Barnett, a resident of Nogales, Arizona,[5] encountered a Barnett family in California whose members told him that they were descendants of a British family which had migrated to Virginia in the 1840s and had moved to California in 1849. They said there were three sons: John, born in 1823; James, born in 1831; and William, born in 1832, who had left home in California and had never been heard from since. The story closely parallels our William's account except for the names of his parents. On family birth certificates he gave their names as William Barnett and Delves Silles[6]. The names given by the California family were John and Rebecca.[7]

The two accounts have so much in common, nevertheless, that they must be describing the same family, but the question remains: Why did William tell such widely different stories? It is possible that he was deliberately trying to make it difficult for anyone to arrive at the facts by claiming to have been born at places as remote as possible from Virginia and California.

It is worth noting that if William had possessed an authentic certificate showing him to have been born in the United States, he could easily have acquired the Mexican citizenship which he never claimed, even though it would have made his life much simpler. He apparently slipped into Mexico, made loyal and influential friends in Sonora, owned and operated one of the state's greatest haciendas, and raised nine sons and two daughters— while remaining himself a foreigner.

Crossing the border and setting up permanent residence in Mexico in the mid-nineteenth century was probably not difficult. Mexico's war with the United States, close on the heels of revolution, had been followed by the War of the Reform and by the French military occupation. Sonorans were preoccupied with the continuing quarrel between Liberal adherents of Ignacio Pesqueira and the Conservatives who supported Manuel Gándara. The appearance of an unassuming and agreeable young Inglés in one of the little mining towns near the Yaqui River in central Sonora probably would have aroused little interest had Romance not entered the picture. When William fell in love with Juana Sánchez, daughter of Valentin Sánchez, however, there was a loud and indignant outcry. The Sánchez family were not ordinary people. Originally from Sinaloa, they were related to Delfina and Amparo Sánchez, who had married Ricardo and Manuel Johnson, developers of the famous silver mines at *Minas Prietas*.[8] Sánchez, apparently determined that his daughter should not sully the family escutcheon by marrying a gringo, sent Juana to Sinaloa to be under the watchful eye of her half-sister Socorro.

William was equal to the occasion. He followed Juana to Sinaloa and, with the surreptitious aid of "someone in the house," he arranged her escape and "deposited" her in a convent to await her impending majority.

After they married, they made their home in Rosario, Sinaloa, where their first son, José, was born in or about 1864. Their first daughter, Adelaida, was born in Durango approximately two years later. They were neither prosperous nor happy in the high mountains of that state, however, and Juana — according to family tradition — repeated an old saying to her husband: "*A tu tierra, grulla; que esta no es la tuya.*" ([Return] to your own land, crane; this is not yours). And so they returned to the lower Sonora River valley and made their home in the Villa de Seris, a former presidio across the river from Hermosillo.

Life there was for a while a struggle. While her husband scouted for business opportunities, Juana pawned some earrings to buy flour and sugar and opened a home bakery. Family tradition again has it that she originated "coyotas," brown-sugar cookies which still are available at Villa de Seris. Before many months, William was operating an export-import business and had begun to acquire property in the Hermosillo area. Slate tax records indicate that in the mid-1870s he had begun to prosper.[9]

William Barnett

Juana Sanchez Barnett

Some, at least, of his prosperity he owed to the establishment of the firm and long-lasting friendships which are generally supposed to have facilitated his circumvention of the law in acquiring and holding La Arizona. One such friendship was with Ramón Corral, journalist, author, governor of Sonora (1888), and vice-president of the Mexican Republic during the last two terms of President Porfirio Díaz (1904, 1910). When in the mid-1870s Corral, having publicly attacked the Pesqueira faction in his newspaper during a state election campaign, was forced to flee for his life, William hid the fugitive in a warehouse, then smuggled him out of the state hidden in a wagonload of freight. Thirty-five years later, when William's son Alberto was unable to collect a sizeable debt, a letter to Corral soon brought a settlement in Alberto's favor.

The exact date of William's acquisition of La Arizona has been impossible to determine—and with good reason. According to Mexican law, no foreigner could own land within 80 kilometers (approximately fifty miles) of the border; neither could the wife of a foreigner acquire such land. William's wife, in fact, "denounced" (claimed) a piece of land adjoining La Arizona in 1881, but her claim was rejected for this reason.[10] In some instances, notably in the case of William C. Greene in Cananea and William Randolph Hearst in the same general area, special permits issued by the federal government nullified the prohibition. Such was not the case at La Arizona, however, and the property remained in the names of William's friends until his sons came of age.

The *Real de Arizonac* had been established in 1730 by the *alcalde mayor* of Sonora. In 1736 the flurry of mining after discovery of the *Planchas de Plata* was soon dissipated, and because of its remoteness, the difficult surrounding terrain, and the Apache menace, the area was totally depopulated during the first half of the 19th century. Then, in 1850, records show that twenty-four *sitios* (approximately 104,000 acres) were granted to Juan B. Gándara, Rafael Buelna, Manuel Monteverde, Florencio Monteverde, and Celedonio Ortiz.[11] Gándara. congressional representative and brother of Manuel Gándara. ex-governor of Sonora, would die the following year of cholera morbus. The remaining grantees would attain important places in the economic and political life of the state. It is perhaps noteworthy that Ortiz and Monteverde were also close friends of Ramón Corral. There can be no doubt that these were the same lands encompassed in La Arizona, and the means by which William acquired possession in the 1870s were very likely the same by which he later gained control of the land Juana was to claim in 1881. Records show that immediately after rejection of her claim, William's old friends Celedonio Ortiz and Florencio and Manuel Monteverde denounced the same property and the transaction was approved.[12] In both cases they simply held title until

William's Mexican-born sons were old enough to assume it.

Whatever the date of acquisition, William apparently took up residence on La Arizona, leaving Juana to mind the store in the Villa while he got the place in shape. Alberto, William's third son, remembered that he was taken to live there at the age of five in 1876. This would seem to imply that not only had the ranch been improved but a house had been built.

Juana, with the six children including Arturo, born in Hermosillo in 1873, and Carlos, less than a year old, moved to the ranch also, but returned to Hermosillo for Enrique's birth in 1877 and again for Carmen's in 1879. In 1882 she suffered severe complications in giving birth to a girl child at La Arizona. A rider was dispatched over the primitive river road to Saric, twelve miles west, to fetch a priest; Juana died and shortly afterward so did the child. They were buried in the little *campo santo* on the hill behind the house.

After Juana's death, William had three sons by Dolores Badilla, daughter of Miguel and Jesús Leon Badilla of Horcasitas. She had come to the ranch originally as a housekeeper, but although William acknowledged the children, he never married Dolores. While the boys were still very young, she left the Big House, probably because of the objections of William's older sons, and Carmen became a surrogate mother to her half-brothers. Dolores remained at La Arizona, however, and eventually was also buried in the *campo santo*.

Meanwhile, William had become an important cattle rancher. According to one of his grandsons, at one time he was supplying jerked beef to the Mexican navy at the rate of twenty head per day. He also exported cattle to the United States and was raising, among other livestock, sheep and geese, horses and honey bees. Wheat, corn, vegetables, sugar cane, orchard fruits, and strawberries also were produced. But perhaps the secret of his outstanding success was the processing of the natural products at the site of production.

There was a tannery, a soap factory, a small *trapiche* (cane sugar mill), looms on which *serapes* were woven, and a canning factory. The women even made cigarettes for home consumption, cutting paper obtained in Tucson, rolling them by hand, and tying the smokes in bundles.

The *Oasis* (Nogales, A.T.) for November 30, 1895, mentioned the year's production at La Arizona as 3500 cans of peaches, 1500 cans of apples, and 260 cans of pears. The story said William was planning to process evaporated milk. He also sold dried fruits and hams. Wagons were built in the home shop and there was a talabarteria where saddles and harness were made. A store in the Big House sold food to the prospectors who came from neighboring placers and paid with gold dust.

As they grew old enough, William's sons became involved with the business of the ranch and as they married, William built a house for each of them until the home place, nestled between protecting hills and bisected by a clear, burbling stream, came to resemble a small village. The Big House, a one-story adobe structure half as large as a city block, was built in the

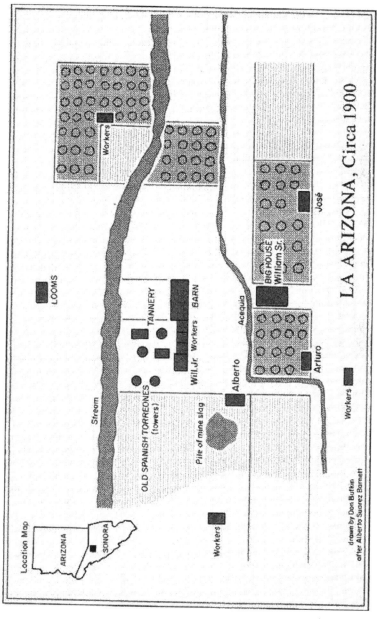

traditional Spanish Colonial style around a patio, with spacious rooms, huge fireplaces, and eighteen-foot ceilings finished with native bamboo laid over the beams. It was situated on a rise overlooking open fields sloping gently down to the cottonwoods along the creek. Small orchards on either side of the house sheltered the homes of Arturo and José. William, Jr. (Guillermo) attached his house to the workers' barracks next to the barn. Alberto built his comfortable home off to the left a few hundred feet.

Incidentally, in the 1890s, when landowners found it expedient to re-survey their holdings in order to substantiate their land claims with the Mexican government, it was discovered that placing twenty-four *sitios* so the northern boundary coincided with the U.S.–Mexico border as stipulated in the claim, left La Arizona's headquarters—and the springs—outside the claim. William then acquired additional property adjoining the original grant on the south and east.[13]

Midway between the Big House and the creek bottom there was a pile of slag believed to be the remainder of a small smelting operation conducted during the early mining days at the real. Two crumbling *torreones* beyond the barn and close to the creek were believed to be relics of the same operation, probably built to protect workers at the smelter from marauding Indians. There is no evidence, however, that William ever made an effort to prospect in the once fabulously rich mineral area, even though the old *Planchas de Plata* was located on his property. Sporadic attempts by others to reopen the mine left him unconcerned because, according to Mexican law, a property owner's "surface rights" were not affected by "mineral rights" of a claimant to a mine.

Ana Barnett, daughter of William's son Alberto, recalled at the age of eighty-four, in 1982, the *torreones* and the slag heap and remembered that as a child she was occasionally taken on a day-long "prospecting trip" to the mineralized area by her Uncle Gregorio. She remembered it as a sort of picnic, however, and believed no one considered prospecting seriously.

Not then, perhaps. But a report on *El Real de La Arizonac* and *Planchas de Plata* made by the governor of Sonora in 1849 at the request of the Interior Department in Mexico City[14] had led to serious consideration of such prospecting by a great number of people. Apparently as a direct consequence of the report, the famous *Compañia Restauradora de la Mina de la Arizona* was formed by Count Gaston de Raousset-Boulbon, an ambitious "California Frenchman" with a thirst for adventure, and the great Franco-Mexican banking house of Jecker, Torre and Company.[15] Raousset-Boulbon was to organize in San Francisco a company of 150 Frenchmen, transport them to

Guaymas, and proceed to the District of Arizona, where they would take possession of lands, mines and placers, deliver to Jecker-Torre the rights to such properties, and "defend same." Ultimately one-half of the properties would go to Raousset and half to *La Restauradora.*

Ruins of the Big House at La Arizona, 1977.

Before the French party arrived, however, Sonoran authorities had second thoughts about having such a large area, in effect, colonized by foreigners and approved, instead, a proposition by a rival company, the *Sociedad Exploradora de Metales de Sonora,* which intended to explore and secure the same territory under protection of the Mexican military.[16]

Raousset arrived with 200 well-armed men and, in defiance of Sonoran authorities, established what amounted to a military headquarters at Saric. When, after attempting to foment an insurrection and refusing to confer with Mexican military authorities, he was ordered to leave, he retaliated by taking the city of Hermosillo after a bloody battle and holding it for nearly a week. In the end, Raousset-Boulbon was felled by an illness and his men, taken prisoner, were shipped back to California.

The French company's defeat was closely followed by ratification of the Gadsden Purchase (which, according to rumor, included most of Sonora) and by an attempted filibuster by the American William Walker. Disheartened by dissension within and alarmed by the threat of invasion, Sonoran authorities encouraged settlement in the border area as a means of preserving the state. William's development of La Arizona would have been consistent with official protective strategy. Although he pretended to have been born in the U.S.A., Sonoran authorities certainly knew he had not been, and after twenty years in the country he could certainly no longer have been considered an immigrant. The state was anti-French, anti-American and anti-immigrant but not anti-English. The Sociedad Exploradora, for example, was British-backed. Occupation of the borderlands was not only a deterrent to would-be colonizers from the north but an essential element in defense against the Apaches.

Some ten years after William had moved his family to the ranch, he was seriously involved in the last Apache campaign. Geronimo's band had swept through southern Arizona in April. 1886, killing rancher Al Peck's wife and child near Calabasas and attacking the ranch of Hank Hewitt and Yank Bartlett near Ruby. Crossing the border, they were followed to the Pinito Mountains by a detachment of the U.S. 10th Cavalry commanded by Captain Thomas C. Lebo and Lieutenants John Bigelow, Jr., and Powhatan H. Clarke.[17] (The Barnetts have preserved a map of Sonora left by Lieutenant Clarke at La Arizona, where a base of operations had been established by both the American and Mexican forces.) Corporal Edward Scott, wounded in a skirmish in the mountains, was boldly rescued by Lieutenant Clarke, for which action the lieutenant later was given the Medal of Honor. The incident was also immortalized in a work by Frederic Remington, who was engaged at the time in doing a series of paintings of the army in action.

The Indians then divided, one group returning to the vicinity of La Arizona, where they were attacked by Mexican troops from the Altar District and from the Magdalena District.[18] Employing guerrilla tactics, including burning the grass to turn the enemy, the Indians took many of the Mexicans' horses and left several dead including two American prospectors, J. Sullivan and D. McCarty, and a courier of William Barnett. Alberto, then fifteen years of age, remembered being in the party that discovered the bodies. When General Nelson Miles sent additional troops by train to Agua Zarca, from which a trail led to the ranch, the Indians fled to the high mountains again and, except for one final raid in June, when the Indians stole several horses from a field immediately adjoining the house, peace returned to La Arizona.

For more than two decades, then, life for William's family apparently continued at a measured pace—not idyllic, perhaps, but certainly in an aura of stability and contentment. About a year after Juana's death William had taken Dolores as his common-law wife and their first son was born at La Arizona in 1884. The second, born eighteen months later during the Apache campaign, was appropriately named Geronimo. The third, Ricardo, was born in 1888. By the turn of the century, Alberto, Arturo, Guillermo, and José were married and living in their own homes. Alberto married Virginia Gaxiola, great-granddaughter of Clemencia Sánchez, who was a distant relative of Juana Sánchez.[19] Virginia's father died in Fronteras at the hands of the Apaches during the last Geronimo campaign in 1886. Enrique married Maria Luisa Pierson, granddaughter of a French physician who, although he had not supported Maximilian's empire, had been forced to flee with a group of suspected sympathizers. He was captured and wrongfully executed after the French defeat.[20]

William, although living in comparative isolation and in a thoroughly self-sufficient manner, never became a recluse. According to Ana, he made several pleasure trips to the U.S. He visited the Columbian Exposition in Chicago and was accompanied by his daughter Carmen on one of his trips to San Francisco. He also made regular business trips to Tucson, staying, while in town, at the home of his old friend Albert Steinfeld. He was obviously well-known in northern Sonora and his name appeared occasionally in the weekly paper in Nogales, Arizona. In November, 1885, he found it necessary to write a letter to the editor of *La Constitución*, a Hermosillo paper,[21] protesting what he called a totally unfounded story that he had sold 1,500 *novillos* (steers) to a butcher in Tucson, a quantity which evidently would have exceeded legal export-import limitations. He said he had sold 115 *novillos* and, "as true as the 1,500 *novillos* is what is said about the Arizona Ranch." Unfortunately, all efforts to locate the newspaper to learn what was said about the ranch have not been successful. The paper also mentioned that in July, 1885, one Guillermo Benit was tried for falsifying the signature of Guillermo Barnett in attempting to buy on credit merchandise in a store in Hermosillo. It was also reported on January 24, 1884, that William had contributed toward establishment of a school in Hermosillo.

On La Arizona William had established a school for his own children and those of employees on the ranch. Ana remembers that it was conducted in the home of José and presided over by the elderly "Don Leandrito," who was eventually replaced by Doña Simona Aguilera, a native of Guadalajara.

Previously, Alberto at a very early age had been sent to Orb Blanco. (Old Oro Blanco, the first settlement, was situated in the United States but very close to the international line and only about ten miles due north of the Big House at La Arizona.) There he studied at a little school that Dr. Adolphus H. Noon had established for his sons. Later, Alberto liked to tell a tale about his being so fond of milk that he used to raid the kitchen in the dark and drink the supply the cook had set aside for his morning coffee. One night the cook caught him in the act and, to shame him, cut off a tuft of his hair. Alberto, then, to cover his crime, sneaked into the Noon boys' bedroom and cut off tufts of hair from each of their heads. He didn't say how Dr. Noon reacted. To further Alberto's education, William then sent him to Tucson, where he lived with the Steinfelds and worked at the store while continuing his studies.

At the ranch, the family lived well. There were homemade cider and fruit wines, dried and preserved fruits, honey in the comb and a smokehouse hung with hams and other meats. Pillows were stuffed with goose down and blankets were woven of lamb's wool. As his sons assumed more and greater responsibilities, William, although always in command, found time for relaxation and reflection. Ana remembers him sitting on the veranda mornings in the shade of the giant cottonwoods, reading and smoking with the two dogs, Fanny and Benny, at his feet.

The unrest preceding the Revolution of 1910 infected all of northern Sonora, including La Arizona. Guillermo, Jr., moved his family to a house on *Avenida Obregon* a few blocks from the international line in Nogales, Sonora. He persuaded his ailing father to share his new home and there William died on October 7, 1909, at the age of about eighty-one.

Some of William's sons—among them, Alberto—had sent their sons to school on the American side, first to Nogales, where nuns were conducting a school in the old Camou house at Arroyo Blvd. and Walnut St., and later to Tucson. When the revolution became disruptive in Nogales, Sonora, several of the brothers themselves moved across the line. Later they returned to Mexico but never to the ranch. After the assassination of President Francisco Madero in February, 1913, Guillermo, Jr., then mayor of Nogales, Sonora, resigned and moved to Nogales, Arizona.

Ana and her sisters were born in a small house on Sonoita Avenue in Nogales, Arizona, where her mother, Prisciliana, wife of Jesús Gaxiola, had lived since 1890. The house was one of four newly built by Josef Piskorski, whom Ana remembered as an elderly rancher who owned the Piskorski Building on Morley Avenue and "many houses." When he was in town, however, he stayed in a "room in the back," where he was found dead of food poisoning one morning. The house (still standing) overlooked the heart of Ambos Nogales and Ana remembers seeing revolutionary soldiers with cattle which she recognized as belonging to La Arizona.

The ranch was sold to the West Coast Cattle Company, probably in 1915, and in 1919 cattleman and entrepreneur Joseph Wise of Calabasas and Nogales, Arizona, accepted title to the ranch as repayment of a loan he had made to the company.[22] Joseph's son, the late Knight Wise, managed the ranch and made his home there for many years. His son Pepe was still running the place in 1981 while maintaining a part-time home in Nogales.

More than half the great hacienda has been confiscated by the Mexican government and is presently an *ejido*, a communal agricultural operation concerning which there is endless controversy. Except for Pepe's starkly modern home adjacent to the site of the former Big House, the houses have crumbled and returned to earth. Fences and outbuildings are in good repair, however, and the great cottonwoods still stand. The crystal stream, hurrying from the living springs of Arizonac to the sea, must look much as it did when William and his young wife first brought their family and their hopes to La Arizona on the Mexican frontier.

NOTES

[1] Intimate details of family life at La Arizona were given by Ana Burnett to her nephew Alberto Suarez Barnett (co-author) in several interviews during the summer of 1981. p. 124.

[2] Birth certificate of Leonor Barnett, *Registro Civil del Estado*, Hermoslllo, Sonora. *ibid.*

[3] Birth certificate Alejandro Barnett, *ibid.*

[4] Letter to the U.S. Consul, Nogales, Sonora, File no. 221, BZ/agu. *ibid.*

[5] Jerry Barnett, interviews with Alberto Suarez Barnett, Nogales, June, 1981. *ibid.*

[6] Birth certificate of Carmen Barnett, *Registro Civil del Estado.* Hermosillo. Sonora. *ibid.*

[7] Jerry Barnett, interviews with Alberto Suarez Barnett. *ibid.*

[8] Lic. Luis Encinas Johnson, interview Alberto Suarez Barnett, Hermosillo, Sonora, November, 1981. p. 115.

[9] *La Estrella del Occidente* (Hermosillo), II Epoca, May 10. 1872; December 15. 1873; November 3, 1876; January 30. 1879. p. 116.

[10] *La Constitución* (Hermosillo), August 8, 1881. p. 117.

[11] *Titulos de Terrenos que existen en la Tesoreria General del Estado Pertenecientes a Sonora & Sinaloa* (Hermosillo, Sonora: *Imprenla del Estad*, 1889). *ibid.*

[12] *La Constitución*, April 12, 1882. *ibid.*

[13] Map of twenty-four *sitios* of La Arizona made by Ignacio Bonillas, Nogales, Arizona Territory, December 1. 1889. *ibid.*

[14] Historical Archives of the Gov. of Sonora, volume 220, Hermosillo. Sonora. p. 120.

[15]Rufus Kay Wyllys, *The French in Sonora* (Berkley: University of California Press. 1932), *ibid.*

[16]*Ibid.*, p. 121.

[17]Jack C Gale, "Lebo in Pursuit," *Journal of Arizona History*, vol. 21 (Spring, 1980). p. 122.

[18]*La Constitución*, May 11, 21, and June 25. 1886. *ibid.*

[19]Gaxiola family. Book of Births and Deaths, in possession of Alberto Suarez Barnett. p. 123.

[20]Jerry Barnett, interviews with Alberto Suarez Barnett. *ibid.*

[21]*La Constitución*, November 26, 1885. *ibid.*

[22]Marguerite Wise Macdonald, interview with Alma Ready, Nogales, Arizona, October, 1981. p. 125.

CREDITS: The photographs on page 116 are from the Ana Barnett collection; on page 121 from the Alma Ready collection.

AFTERWORD

by Patrick D. Simpson

Let me start from the beginning…

On December 17, 1907, four years to the day after the Wright brothers made the first of four controlled airplane flights over the sands of Kitty Kawk, my mother was born as Alma Henderson Duffield in Cedarville, a little village located along the Delaware Bayshore on the southern tip of New Jersey. Over the next 95 years – sandwiched between two memorable boyfriends – she made four sustained flights of her own. Flights into marriage, that is – the last being the longest. Four marriages, four name changes, four children – all boys.

So please allow me introduce myself… My full name is Patrick Duffield Simpson and I am the first of two sons from my mother's third marriage. From the time I was five, my brother Jim and I grew up in the little town of Sidney, New York while Mom – who by now had again remarried – lived in far off Arizona. Jim and I were raised by my father, Raymond Simpson, with help – lots of help – from my grandparents Jay C. and "Mamie" Simpson.

My last name has always been Simpson but my much-married mother has had five last names. She had so many addresses during her lifetime that I regularly had to white-out my address book to keep current. But her final last name – Ready – was the one she carried throughout her Arizona writing career – the last 48 of her 95 years.

Mom gave me three brothers, one of whom I grew up and two longtime strangers with different last names. I can't speak for the others but the one constant in my life has always been the love I've had for my mother. I'll never forget her willingness to help this neophyte writer back in the late 1990's. By the end of her life, we had become re-acquainted – even close friends.

But I'm getting ahead of myself.

On one of our late-in-life trips together – a jaunt into northern Arizona and Wahweap Lodge on Lake Powell, she showed me a copy of her recently completed manuscript, MEMOIR. I didn't see it again until shortly after her death in 2003. Her boyfriend/caregiver, Frank Light, helped me collect her effects, among which were a good many photographs, awards and writings, including the aforementioned MEMOIR.

Raymond never remarried, but he tried his best to give us a good start in life. As a young man he'd graduated from the Eastman Business College in Poughkeepsie, New York; later, at a police school in New York City. He also became a journeyman toolmaker at "Scintilla", Sidney's large Bendix Corporation plant. All this training served him well in later years as a plant protection officer, mainly in charge of the main gate where all the VIPs signed in and out.

On March 31, 1967, Raymond Simpson retired as Security officer from Bendix Corporation's Scintilla Division in Sidney, New York.

A threesome - Pat (l.). Raymond, Jim

Sidney Town Band - 1950s

He kept us in school and in Sunday school at the Sidney Methodist Church. He loved to fish and camp; he took us on several camping trips into the Adirondacks (Brown Tract Pond, NY), sometimes even into Canada (Calabogie Lake, Ontario and Lac Témiscamingue, Quebec). He was active in the local Masonic Lodge and, for most of his life, played trombone in the town band. By 1970, due to declining health, he'd moved into our home. Raymond died in 1971 of a stroke and heart attack. He was only 69.

Jim: Both Jim and I graduated from Sidney Central High School; I in 1956, he in 1958. At school I was the "nonconformist" – Jim, the "superstar." He was an outstanding member of the All Star basketball team all through high school. And that's not all – he was a member of both the Honor Society and Student Council, and – junior and senior class president.

With help from a General Motors Scholarship Jim went on to Colgate University where he joined the Phi Delta Theta fraternity and majored in Russian studies more than sports. He eventually earned an A.B. (equivalent to B.A.) in Russian Studies and an M.A. in Education (Teaching of Social Studies).

In 1962, only two months after graduation, Jim married the beautiful Adrienne Matteson, an Oneonta State student from Franklin, N.Y. The two had met as fellow summer employees at Scott's Oquaga Lake House, a Catskill summer resort near Deposit, N.Y. They moved west 45 miles to Whitney Point, N.Y. where Jim taught ninth grade geography at Whitney Point Central School. By 1967, they'd moved another 75 miles west, this time to Horseheads, N.Y., where Jim began a new role as guidance counselor in Horseheads Junior High School. By now, they had two children: Steven and Colleen.

On August 24, 1968. I got a call from Horseheads in the middle of the night. A voice – I don't remember who – said: "Mr. Simpson, I'm very sorry I have to tell you this, but your brother Jim has died."

I didn't believe it. I still don't believe it. Jim had died tragically in his automobile. He was only 28. We grew up together. We were *always* together.

All-Star Contests Won by "North"
Sidney Record-Enterprise
Thursday, March 1, 1956

Sidney Record-Enterprise, Thursday, March 1, 1956: WELL-EARNED HONORS—Here are the best of the two Sidney squads: Frank Mitrzyk and Dave Ineich of the Varsity squad and James Simpson and Dick Almy representing the JV.

Led by Basil Anagnost and Jim Simpson, the Northern Division of the Susquenango League swept the All-Star contest in both the Varsity and Junior Varsity star studded contests. Anagnost led the Northern squad with 21 counters in a 77-56 rout of the South and Jim Simpson tossed in a 21-foot set shot with 10 seconds left to win for the North JV, 50 to 47. Simpson also had 10 points to pace the winners.

But that's not the end of the story…

Four years later, Adrienne married a man whom I can only call great. Yes, Chet was a *great* man. Although we lived miles apart, Chester "Chet" Silvernail seemed like another brother to me. He and Adrienne did an absolutely remarkable job raising my nephew and niece. I often told him, "Chet, if it wasn't meant for Jim to raise those kids, I can't think of a better man than you." Adrienne and Chet stayed married until he died at their farm in Greene, New York in 2012. He was 76. God bless you, Chet and Adrienne, for being a constant inspiration to us all

Chet & Adrienne at their farm, May 2009.

Don: It wasn't until 28 years after Jim's death – July 9, 1996 – that I first met Mom's first son, Donald Flowers. I was 57, he was 66. The happy reunion occurred as Anne and I were returning to Raleigh from an Oregon research trip for my third book: *Whither Thou Goest*. Don's home was in Novi, Michigan (pop. 47,000) a city about 25 miles northwest of Detroit. We found him waiting for us in his driveway. We were both a little nervous: after all, what do you say to a long-lost brother whom you've never met?

But there was nothing to fear – after a big hug we headed toward the house. Don looked pretty good – white hair and all – for a man who'd already suffered a mild stroke and a heart attack. We soon met his lively wife Gerri, who tried hard to make us feel at home – and succeeded! She took us to their "Florida room" and brought out snacks and drinks. We were soon enjoying a great dinner and chatting like old friends. Gerri's ebullient personality had the effect of relaxing all of us, regardless of worries we may have had about this late-in-life reunion.

From left: Anne Simpson, Gerri & Don Flowers. On floor: Pat Simpson

Afterwards, we swapped life stories in the living room. It turns out that after my mother left his father, Don grew up with a step-mother with whom he never had a great relationship. I don't know if it was because of, or in spite of those early experiences, but Don decided to become a minister. After graduation from the University of Michigan in 1951, he went on to Yale University where he graduated in 1955 with a Bachelor of Divinity degree, one year after his marriage to Gerri.

Over the years, they had four children as Don served as a Presbyterian minister in three churches – specializing in youth counseling. Nevertheless, in 1969 he left the ministry. When I asked why, Don said that the writing was on the wall: congregational membership in the denomination was rapidly dwindling and he didn't want to be one of the 1,500–2,500 ministers who would soon be out of a job. Merrill Lynch hired him as an account executive in Detroit, but eight years later he left to become Vice President in charge of Finance at HR Krueger Machine Tool Company in Farmington, Michigan. He'd retired only months before our visit because of the stroke.

After breakfast the next morning, we parted ways again. I gave Don a big hug and then Anne and I continued south to Raleigh, wondering if – after 57 years of separation – we'd ever see each other again.

We did! Don wanted to reconnect somehow with his family, so he and Gerri later came to two family weddings: my daughter Diana Simpson's marriage to George Feaver on Sept. 7, 2002 in Hartwick, N.Y., and my nephew Steven Simpson's wedding to Shannon Slingerland on Oct. 12, 2003 in Genoa, Ohio. None too soon – In less than a year (August 31, 2004), Don had another stroke; he died at home in Novi. Don never saw Mom again, but he had reconnected – at last – with at least *some* missing parts of his life.

Don and Gerri at Diana's wedding (left) and at Steven's wedding.

John: (Psalm 69:8 *I am a foreigner to my own family, a stranger to my own mother's children.*)

On July 22, 1996, only two weeks after I first met Don, I had another reunion – this time a very sad one – with my other half-brother, John Ready, whom I'd seen but once since the late 1970s – at his Oak Road home in Snellville, Georgia. Mom called me with the sad news: John's wife, the former Carole Sue Harris, had just died from lung cancer in Eastside Medical Center, not far from their home in Snellville. She was only 49.

Two days later, Anne and I found ourselves at the Tom M. Wages funeral home in Snellville where Carole's memorial service was about to begin. There were more than a hundred people present, none of whom – except for John – had we ever seen before.

Carole Sue Harris was only eleven days younger than John. They had first lived in Arizona, where – for six years – he'd worked as a supervisor in Pima

Mines south of Tucson. They later moved to Georgia, where he held supervisory positions at Atlantic Steel, the Vulcan Materials Company and the Georgia Marble Company. In addition, he'd been running an auto repair shop for 25 years out of their home in Snellville.

We soon met Carole's two daughters, Shannon Slocum (now Gleason) with husband Warren and months-old son Johnathan; and Cathy Lester, with husband Jim and two sons: Chris (12) and Adam (9). Adam reminded me of John at that age.

As the service began, it was easy to see by the faces of friends and acquaintances that Carole was indeed an extraordinary woman. Rob, her manager at LXE Telecommunications (a branch company of the first company she'd worked for: Wang, one of the *first* computer companies) gave the first eulogy. He spoke more than eloquently about "Mom" Carole, who "ran things better than anyone else, and was known lovingly as everybody's mom." Then Shannon stood and read a beautiful poem she'd written, mentioning how glad her mother was to have seen her two daughters get

Happier days.

Johnathan Slocum

Shannon's wedding day (Feb. 1995). From left: sister, Cathy Lester; father, John Ready; Shannon Slocum (nee Ready); and Cathy's sons, Adam & Chris Lester. Shannon's mother, Carole Ready (upper right). died on July 22, 1996, four days after Johnathan's 1st birthday. Inset: Johnathan Slocum, born July. 1995.

married (see photo above) and to see all three grandsons. Shannon held up right to the end as tears flowed soundlessly down her cheeks.

Afterwards, we went back to John's home – now located on Statewood Court – where Cathy and Shannon had prepared a remarkable buffet of ravioli, salad, bread, drinks and dessert for the family. We talked and talked until it was time to go. John told me that he had lost his "soul mate". I told him that even if his soul *had* been torn apart, that God could restore it.

Anne and I never got back to our motel until midnight; the Summer Olympics were already underway in Atlanta and the closest affordable room we could find was in Athens, Georgia, about an hour away.

By morning we were gone. I never saw any of them again, but every now and then, John and I would talk on the phone – although rarely.

And then – in late February of 2015 – something urged me to call him again – perhaps just to see if he was still alive. And he was! We had a nice talk about where he'd lived, what he was doing, how he was feeling, how he'd learned to hunt from his dad.

Ted taught Johnny camping and how to fish and hunt. Alma took the pictures.
Photos courtesy of John's daughter, Shannon Ready Gleason.

And, for the first time, I learned he was still being treated by the V.A. for exposure to Agent Orange in Vietnam while serving in the U.S. Air Force. (Axel Holm, who wrote the foreword to this book, had met John as they trained together at Lowry Air Force Base, Colorado.)

On Monday, March 30, 2015, I received a call from Shannon. John had died at home in Snellville on March 18 – an abdominal aneurysm, probably brought on by the aforementioned Agent Orange. A private memorial had been held in his home on Saturday, only two days before Shannon's call. It wasn't until afterwards, she said, while sorting through his papers, that she'd found my address and phone number.

So now we're sharing photos and memories together, each grieving in our own way. God bless you, little brother.

I know it's not fair without family and the memories we shared.
There's nothing that we could do to bring time back.
I just want you to know we love you no matter where you are.

— from "Absent Brother" © Kimberly Barry, January 2008

John Ready (center), three days before his death, with daughter Shannon (r.) and grandson Johnathan.

Buddies: By 1995, I'd actually written a draft version of my first book, *Wheelchair Around the World.* Not knowing what to expect after years of separation, I called my mother and asked, "Mom, would you proofread it for me?" Without hesitation and much to my relief, she said "Yes." So I mailed it to her and she returned it, section by section, with all changes, suggestions and errors meticulously written or underlined in red. From that moment on, we became "buddies."

Afterwards, I thought, "What was I afraid of? Rejection? After all, she had in effect rejected all her sons but John, the one she'd actually raised." I could have let anger and resentment eat away at me and be 100 percent justified, but I'd be the one left paying the price because I'd let another person make me miserable.

No. I had decided to forgive her. Forgiveness is not a feeling; it's a choice you consciously make. As a Christian, I rejoiced that God had forgiven my sins. Who was I then not to forgive my own mother? There is some good in the worst of us and some bad in the best of us.

And when I think about it, perhaps Mom – one time church organist and glee club president – while claiming to be an agnostic, had deep inside sought forgiveness from God and from at least one of her children. She'd found it from me. – I prayed she would also find it from God.

Over the next few years, I would visit her from Raleigh as much as I could; Anne joined me more than once. Mom always wanted to show me "her" West and did so at every opportunity.

Frank: Teddy had died ten years before but Mom now had a new boyfriend – ten years younger than herself. Handsome Frank E. Light was a U.S. Navy veteran, a New England transplant since 1976, a Nogales humanitarian – and a widower. He was a member of the Lions Club and served on the Nogales Homeowners Association Board as President, Vice-President and Treasurer. He lived in a very nice home, not far from Mom, on a hilltop that overlooked Mr. C's Supper Club. I instantly liked the man.

1988: At 80, Alma shows no sign of slowing down on 3-mile hike with Pat in Arizona's Fort Bowie National Historic Site.

But Frank didn't join us on road trips. I didn't know why – perhaps Mom wanted "family time". I usually drove while Mom navigated – from Nogales day trips into Mexico to overnight trips north into Hopi/Navajo country and Lake Powell. She was tireless! Once, we even did a three-mile round-trip hike together at the Fort Bowie National Historic site. (She was in her eighties and a member of a local hiking club!)

I was always amazed at the historical running commentary she would give us wherever we went – things like: "That's the Apache warpath"; "Over there is the 'Dove of the Desert' (San Xavier Mission)"; "That's Pete Kitchen's ranch just ahead." We visited Spanish missions, Mexican courtyards, copper mines and Old West mining towns. She introduced us to our first chimichangas. We drove for endless miles on bumpy roads, even over Montezuma Pass (elevation 6,575 ft.) in Arizona's Coronado National Memorial. Driving didn't tire her, it exhilarated her. Whenever I grew weary, Mom would take the wheel, driving at 70 mph for miles at a time.

2002, at Carondelet Holy Cross Hospital. Clockwise: Alma Ready, Pat Simpson, Frank Light, Anne Simpson, Lucy Hancock.

The last time I saw Mom was at the Carondelet Holy Cross Hospital in Nogales. She was 95 and had been an Alzheimer's patient for several months.

Needless to say, she had slowed down considerably. Late one night, May 29, 2003, I got the inevitable phone calls – first from the hospital, then from Frank. Mom had died in her sleep. Pneumonia.

How final. I was stunned. I didn't know what to say or do, so I didn't say or do much of anything. I knew that things would never be the same again.

Frank mentioned that Mom had made pre-paid funeral arrangements – including cremation. And, there would be a memorial service sometime soon.

For the next couple of days, I helped Frank work with Nogales's Adair Funeral Home with the funeral arrangements. I even wrote the obituary. Axel Holm, then president of the Pimeria Alta Historical Museum, planned the memorial service. It would be at the museum.

REMEMBERING ALMA

The service was indeed held three weeks later, on the 21st of June. Anne and I flew from Raleigh to Phoenix, and then drove south 180 miles by rental car to Nogales via Tucson.

Abe Rochlin and Susan Clark Spater

From start to finish we could see plumes of smoke spewing from the lofty forests of Tucson's Mount Lemmon. People were calling it "the Aspen Fire" and from a distance it looked like a volcano eruption;. The out-of-control flames had already destroyed over 200 homes.

The day was historic in so many other ways as well: I'll never forget my mother's memorial service, held on the main floor of the very museum she'd helped found.

Former museum director Susan Clark Spater was there as well as former mayor (1959-1965) Abe Rochlin, Mom's friend, who'd helped her to research and write the Nogales Centennial book. Among her other friends were museum curator Teresa Leal, Helen B. Littlefield and Sharon Littlefield, who used to take care of Mom's cats.

Axel Holm had organized the whole thing. At 4:00 p.m., we sat in rows of folding chairs and he began the service by joking "The pastor is too ill to come but he told me I could do it, being baptized at the age of 42." And he did a wonderful job. He began by leading us in unison with prayer and the 23rd Psalm.

Then the eulogies began. It was the most heartfelt and eye-opening part of the service for me: a real tribute to my mom. It was so moving to hear what others thought about her. I had not grown up with Mom but their memories were fast becoming my own. *If only her other sons were here to hear this*, I thought. *If only…*

First up was Lillian Hoff, founder of Santa Cruz County Young Audiences and the Santa Cruz County 1904 Courthouse Preservation Commission. She

Lillian Hoff

reminisced how, when county staff moved to a new complex, Mom had helped her save the 1904 Courthouse ("The Old Lady of Court Street"). "Alma is to be credited," she said, "for her years of dedication in single-handedly tracking down all the necessary documentation required to place the 1904 Courthouse on the National Register of Historic Places on December 7, 1977. Thanks to Alma, the Courthouse was saved and restored. It later housed the Arizona Rangers Museum, the Arizona Cowbelles Museum and the Nogales branch of Cochise Community College."

Then it was my turn. I first thanked Frank for all he'd done for Mom these last few years. (I think he was still very much in love with her.) Then I said, "Mom told me that not long after she had turned 90, a pastor had led her to the Lord. Afterwards, she often spoken of seeing angels."

(pds: Mom had come a long way from the opinion she'd written to me some 27 years earlier:

"I do think a child should have some sort of religious education, although I don't think it matters whether it is Catholic, Protestant or Buddhist. Personally, I believe in the brotherhood of man and the ten commandments but for myself I don't feel the need for organized religion. I do understand that a great many people need to belong to a group and for them church is fine. I'm just not a group person...I'm not an atheist, just sort of a cross between an agnostic and a free thinker. But I may as well add right now that when anyone attempts to make me see the light their way, it puts my back up.")

Susan Spater followed up by reading inspirational Bible verses from the book of Isaiah. She had traveled all the way from her Tucson home this morning by bus – just to be with Alma.

Teresa Leal told about her days of working with Mom and of their mutual interest in all things Santa Cruz County. She announced that the museum's large research library was being renamed the Alma D. Ready Library.

In a special presentation, a beautiful stone plaque, created by Mexican artist Alonzo Villanueva, was mounted at the library entrance. It featured a windmill taken from one of Mom's photographs. She would have loved it.

June 21, 2003 (l-r): Artist Alonzo Villanueva, Axel Holm (Director, Pimeria Alta Historical Society), Teresa Leal (Curator).

Someone had set up several tables of snacks, sandwiches and cookies. Amazingly, even though Mom had outlived most of her contemporaries, nearly forty people – friends, admirers, co-workers and several young people – had come to pay their respects.

(l-r:) **Julie Castillo, Kathleen Escalada (future president of Pimeria Alta Society), Terry Rodriguez**

These young volunteers from Nogales, Sonora/Arizona came to help out.

(l-r:) Anita Lichter, Lillian Hoff, Helen B. Littlefield, Sharon Littlefield.

Scene from the video "Profiles from the Pimeria Alta": Patrick Simpson (l.) with interviewer Axel Holm. (Videotaped in Pimeria Alta Museum's Alma D. Ready Library for the Arizona Historical Society.)

I'll be forever thankful to Axel Holm, who did an incredible job of arranging the service and the reception. Still later, he put on a videotape of our October interview. At the time, he was doing his "Profiles from the Pimeria Alta" video series for the museum and for the Arizona Historical Society. In it he said, "Alma's books are probably one of the greatest gifts that has ever been given to this community."

In July, Frank and Sarah Littlefield scattered Mom's ashes in the hills above the San Rafael Valley, some ninety minutes east of Nogales via Patagonia. It was where Mom had scattered Ted's ashes some seventeen years before.

Frank wrote to me with the following directions:

San Rafael Valley - photo by Alma Ready.

"From Nogales take route 82 (Patagonia Highway) north-east to Patagonia. In Patagonia turn right at the old railroad station, then turn left (about 200 feet) on Harshaw Road. Follow this road about 5 miles until you come to a crossroad. Turn left and go 6 to 7 miles (may not be exact) on San Rafael Valley Road. You will come up a hill and the valley will open up to you. Take the first road to the right and go about 300 feet. Turn left about 100 feet. We spread the ashes in this area."

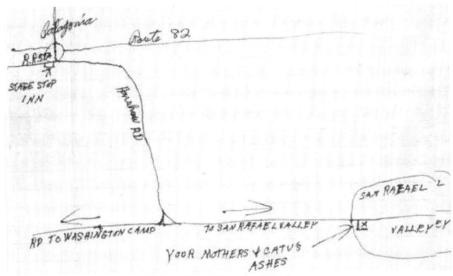

Map by Frank Light.

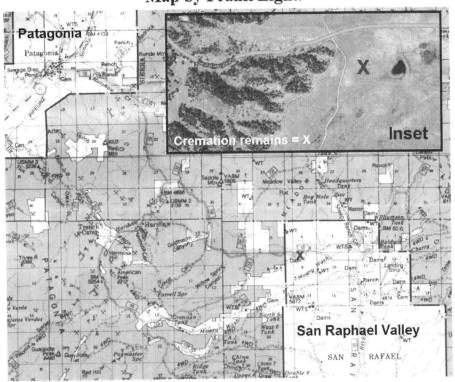

Map with inset, by Patrick Simpson.

Frank, by the way, died in Nogales August 21, 2005 – only two years after Mom. He is buried in the Rose Hill Cemetery at Rock Hill, Connecticut – home of his son Paul. Frank was very much a kind and caring man – a real gentleman.

Mom had many friends in Nogales and was a lover of art, music, poetry and everything Arizona. She will be deeply missed by not only me, but the many people whose lives she has touched over the years. About Nogales she wrote: "I have been very happy here. The country is beautiful, the 'Border Culture' fascinating, the people friendly, and the climate near-perfect. This is where I feel at home."

They say that home is where the heart is. Mom's heart had indeed found a home in Arizona. And my heart has found forgiveness and love for Alma Ready, my mother – my "buddy".

I love you, Mom!

ALMA'S ALMANAC

● For Alma Ready long-time hobby becomes career.

Nogales International (February 1, 1974), (p. 3)

The work of photo-journalist Alma Ready will appear in the *Nogales International* in a monthly photo feature.

Photography, long her prize-winning hobby, and writing have become a new career for Alma at an age when most people are planning retirement.

She came to Nogales to research Santa Cruz County for a year, stayed six, and has resolved to remain for life.

Forthright and determined, Alma is not given to fragile whims.

Taken by the beauty, history and unique quality of Nogales and environs, she said, she now is as firmly cemented as her mobile home in Mariposa.

Open Range and Hidden Silver, on Arizona's Santa Cruz County, is Alma's recently published first book – now almost sold out of the first printing. The result of research which brought her to Nogales, it is a soft-bound collection of striking photos and lively history with sparks of affectionate wit.

Alma was a small town girl from New Jersey where she taught first grade for two years and where her photography began at the age of six.

Waiting to go somewhere one day, she was given a Brownie camera to keep her occupied and tidy until her mother was ready. Her first effort was of a strawberry field in winter, a view she recalls vividly to this day.

Between the strawberry field and her first professional venture for Arizona Highways were years of family album fillers. A separate album was devoted to each long summer camping trip she and husband Theodore took every year from the time their son John was old enough for the adventures. Selections from these expeditions brought her a succession of prizes in Eastman Kodak competition. Alma finally won Tucson area honors in all five categories and a national prize.

Arizona Highways has published her work since November 1962 when her feature on the old mining ghost town of Charleston appeared. She also was a major contributor to the Santa Cruz County Edition of February 1968.

And Alma is Nogales correspondent for the *Phoenix Republic*.

As a liberated senior citizen, she is reveling in the greatest of all luxuries: resisting an imposed schedule and using her time to do what she enjoys most, photography, particularly of the Nogales area.

❂ Historian must dig for Facts like Detective

by John Lemons, Staff Writer
Nogales International (October 25, 1980)

Alma Ready

"Being a historian is a lot like being a detective," said Alma Ready, who has spent the past 13 years digging into the history of Santa Cruz County and Nogales.

Searching through records and newspapers, and talking to people has been her main occupation since she came to Nogales to write a book on local history in 1967, she said.

"There are a lot of people in this area who know more than I do about some particular period, area or event, but the difference is that I can bring it together," she said. "My intent is to try to show how it all developed together — how one thing in one area led to another somewhere else until it became all one fabric woven together."

Since her arrival, she has become one of the authorities on the history of this area and is the author of a history book called *Open Range and Hidden Silver*. She also has written historical articles for several newspapers.

She has been a correspondent for the *Arizona Republic* newspaper in Phoenix for several years and has worked at different times for the *Arizona Daily Star* and the *Nogales International*.

Work at museum

But her most recent contribution to the community has been her work to improve the Pimeria Alta Historical Society's museum, which will be dedicated today. "I have put in an awful lot of hours (at the museum), but I have been so interested in this city's history that it has been worth it," she commented.

Ready became involved with the Historical Society when she moved to Nogales. "After my book came out in 1973, I was elected to the board of directors (of the Historical Society)." Later she was elected as the second vice president.

Museum renovation

During the construction of the new city hall, there had been talk of moving the museum to the old city hall when the city officials moved out, she said. When it was announced that the officials were moving out, the society officially requested the use of the old building, she stated.

Progress toward making the dream a reality was slow and arduous, she explained. A building committee was formed to oversee the renovation.

"I acted as the chairman of the building committee and as a liaison person between the city and society officers," she said. The renovation and organization seemed to drag on forever, she commented, but suddenly someone appeared on the scene who could get the ball moving faster.

"Susan Clark Spater called me and asked if we needed a museum curator," said Ready. "I recognized that she was the one person who could hold this together and get it on the track.

"She just came out of nowhere at just the right moment."

Since then, the museum staff has worked long hours to be ready for today's dedication, she said.

"The one thing that I have realized working here in the museum is how old I am," said Ready, who is 73. Many of the museum artifacts are unknown to the younger people, she complained. "The kids don't know what I am talking about.

"We didn't have a radio, running water or cars when I was a kid. The biggest thrill I had was when I went across the street to listen to the radio through a head set."

New Jersey native

She was born and raised in southern New Jersey and graduated from the New Jersey Teacher's College at Glassboro. "But after teaching elementary school for two years, I resigned."

She then attended the Pierce School of Business in Philadelphia. "I worked most of my adult life as a secretary."

In 1946 she came to Arizona for health reasons and lived in Tucson for 22 years. "I used to come down to this area (Santa Cruz County) camping all the time."

Her affair with the history of Santa Cruz County became a full-time love. Although she has wandered into other parts of Arizona and Mexico in search of the historical threads that run through Nogales, she has continued to live and work here.

Beyond the museum, she has no plans. "Once it (dedication) is over, I am going to Mexico for a week and just lie on the beach," she said.

● Historical Society Offers New Museum-Concept

by John Lemons, Staff Writer
Nogales International (October 25, 1980)

For local historian Alma Ready, today's dedication of the Pimeria Alta Historical Society's new museum represents an improved means to help residents become aware of their cultural and historical heritage.

The dedication will be from 3 until 7 p.m. at the museum on Grand Avenue at Crawford Street.

"A lot of people don't realize what they have here," stated Ready, who is second vice president of the historical society. "History is a lot more than just names and dates."

"The history of this area is a very exciting collection of stories, and they are true. It is exciting enough to make a good television series."

"The new museum will play a new and big role in helping the community become aware of this history," she said. "The museum is no longer a showcase for relics."

"The old-style museum was just a collection of relics in which people went from case to case, looking at objects," she explained. "Many of the items had little meaning to the visitors, and the people working in the museum were sometimes unable to explain the significance of the historical artifacts.

"And after people visited the museum once, they didn't go back because they had seen everything," she added. "Now that will change."

"Most of the historical objects will be stored in the basement and only about a small number will be on display on the main floor at any one time," she explained. "The new system of display will give graphic displays of the people and events that surrounded the use of the relics."

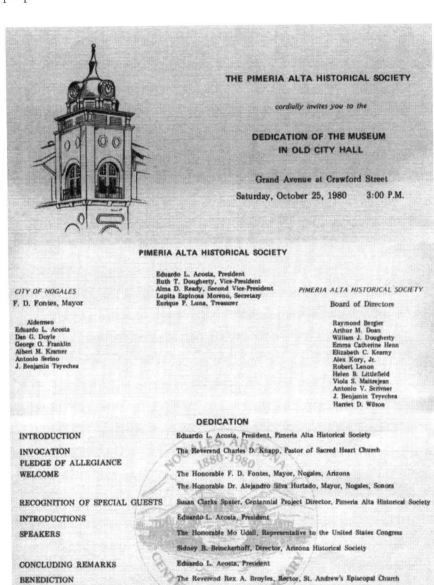

THE PIMERIA ALTA HISTORICAL SOCIETY

cordially invites you to the

**DEDICATION OF THE MUSEUM
IN OLD CITY HALL**

Grand Avenue at Crawford Street
Saturday, October 25, 1980   3:00 P.M.

PIMERIA ALTA HISTORICAL SOCIETY

Eduardo L. Acosta, President
Ruth T. Dougherty, Vice-President
Alma D. Ready, Second Vice-President
Lupita Espinosa Moreno, Secretary
Enrique P. Luna, Treasurer

CITY OF NOGALES
F. D. Fontes, Mayor

Aldermen
Eduardo L. Acosta
Dan G. Doyle
George O. Franklin
Albert M. Kraner
Antonio Serino
J. Benjamin Teyechea

PIMERIA ALTA HISTORICAL SOCIETY

Board of Directors

Raymond Bergier
Arthur M. Doan
William J. Dougherty
Emma Catherine Henn
Elizabeth C. Kearny
Alex Kory, Jr.
Robert Lenon
Helen B. Littlefield
Viola S. Maitrejean
Antonio V. Scrivner
J. Benjamin Teyechea
Harriet D. Wilson

DEDICATION

INTRODUCTION — Eduardo L. Acosta, President, Pimeria Alta Historical Society

INVOCATION — The Reverend Charles D. Knapp, Pastor of Sacred Heart Church

PLEDGE OF ALLEGIANCE

WELCOME — The Honorable F. D. Fontes, Mayor, Nogales, Arizona

The Honorable Dr. Alejandro Silva Hurtado, Mayor, Nogales, Sonora

RECOGNITION OF SPECIAL GUESTS — Susan Clarke Spater, Centennial Project Director, Pimeria Alta Historical Society

INTRODUCTIONS — Eduardo L. Acosta, President

SPEAKERS — The Honorable Mo Udall, Representative to the United States Congress

Sidney B. Brinckerhoff, Director, Arizona Historical Society

CONCLUDING REMARKS — Eduardo L. Acosta, President

BENEDICTION — The Reverend Rex A. Broyles, Rector, St. Andrew's Episcopal Church

RIBBON CUTTING

Immediately following dedication, you are invited to the opening of the Centennial exhibit, 'From Trading Post to Town Hall: Nogales, 1880 - 1915.' Presented by the Pimeria Alta Historical Society with the assistance of the Arizona Historical Society, the exhibit is supported by the Arizona Humanities Council.

"The displays will be changed periodically as new historical themes are presented," said Ready. The Nogales Centennial display is just one example of how this will be accomplished," she added.

"The museum also will be a center where anyone who is interested in history will be able to do research," said Ready. "Although books will not be loaned out, people may come in and read the books that are available in the library."

"A newspaper clipping file also is being established. It will have a subject index, and an ephemera collection will be available for research. The ephemera collection is the filing of maps, publications other than newspapers, research papers and notes by local people," she explained.

The museum is also establishing a collection of taped recordings by local people who want to pass on some of their memories," she added. An active lecture program is also being established to bring area experts from centers of learning such as Tucson and Hermosillo.

The museum's new purpose is to be a community center," said Ready. "It will serve as an educational resource and foster international understanding because of its location."

● Ready is retiring to do more work

by Simon Fisher
Nogales International (January 5, 1983)

Alma Ready retired from the Pimeria Alta Historical Museum last week to work on a project of her own.

Ready is largely responsible for making the museum what it is today. She has worked there since the historical exhibits replaced the bustle of the Nogales City Hall a few years ago when the city moved its offices to the new complex.

"When the city moved out of this building I made it my personal business to get them to let us have it for a museum," she said. "We've been expanding and improving ever since."

After the museum's projects were underway she agreed to organize the library and archives.

"That job is now done," she said as she sat at a large antique desk in the museum's small library.

Shelves full of books cover the walls, each one carefully labeled and catalogued, and an adjacent room is filled with boxes of Nogales' newspapers dating back to the 1800s. Stacks of magazines and manuscripts with the history and photographs of the Pimeria Alta region lie waiting for more shelves to be built.

Alma Ready

"It took an awful long time," she said of the grand effort it took to establish what is often a small research center for historians interested in the people and the land of Southern Arizona and Northwest Sonora.

Tales of the old west came alive when she explained the contents of the books. She spoke of a young lady in the pioneer Pennington family who was captured by the Apaches and thrown off a cliff in the Santa Rita Mountains. The woman landed in a snow bank, survived, and later married and raised a family in Tucson.

She recalled the story of Henry O. Flipper, the first black graduate of West Point who moved west to survey much of the Pimeria Alta region, including the initial mile-square that constituted the city of Nogales in the late 1800s.

Retirement to Alma Ready doesn't mean she will become inactive. Now 75, she said she has retired twice before.

"I will probably act as a consultant for the museum, but I won't keep regular office hours anymore," she said.

She will also work on a collection of photographs of Nogales.

"I'm just going to start taking photos of the Nogales area and see how it turns out. No deadline or subject in mind, just anything that strikes my fancy."

Ready originally came to Nogales from Tucson to work on a book, after retiring from a secretarial job in 1967.

"My hobby was photography and I had a big collection of pictures of this area," she said.

She decided to write a brief history of Santa Cruz County to go with the photographs, but the book took a while to complete because the Arizona Republic needed a reporter in Nogales, and she volunteered for the job.

After more than a dozen years with the Republic, she retired again. The book was published in 1973.

"By that time I had become a native," she said. "I just didn't want to go anywhere else."

With the major part of her work at the museum done, she's on to another project.

But as she'll be working on her photography and occasionally with the museum and the historical society, there will be plenty to keep her busy.

● Friends of The 1904 Courthouse
by Lillian B. Hoff
Nogales Santa Cruz County Magazine – (1993)

Friends of the 1904 Courthouse was chartered February 1991 as a non-profit organization to assist the COURTHOUSE PRESERVATION COMMISSION (CPC) in carrying out its preservation and protection of the Neo-Classical Revival style Santa Cruz County Courthouse and site.

Built in 1904, it is located in downtown Nogales on Morley Avenue. CPC was founded in 1987 in order to assist the Santa Cruz County Board of Supervisors with a bond election to establish a new county complex overlooking the Mariposa corridor, now the center of Nogales.

Concerned citizens, it was felt, would be more prone to vote for a new county complex IF the manifest destiny of the "venerable old lady" on Morley could be assured. That destiny was to preserve and restore the building for adaptive use as a community cultural center.

Now, six years later, the rotunda, recorder's and assessor's offices, are in a beautiful state ready for use. The Santa Cruz County Cowbelles may be the first anchor organization to move in once structural problems and accessibility for the physically challenged are taken care of.

The beautiful turn-of-the-century gas-light replica chandelier hanging in the rotunda with sidelights, are a tribute to the first two zany bed-races undertaken by the author and Chris McLuckie. Chris, formerly of Rio Rico, is now back living in Hawaii where bed-racing originated.

What must be acknowledged, is the fact that sixteen years ago, local writer and historian, Alma Ready, single-handedly placed the 1904 Courthouse on the National Register of Historic Places, December 7, 1977. A former newspaper reporter, Alma is to be credited for her years of dedication in tracking down all the necessary documentation required to place the Courthouse on the Register.

What it comes right down to it is that the purpose of the Friends is to be "Friends in thought, word, and deed", by providing financial and in-kind assistance; preserving and protecting the historic building for future generations to enjoy; and overseeing adaptive use for fine arts, crafts, and other community use. That's a large order!

IN RECOGNITION OF ITS CONTRIBUTION
TO THE CULTURAL HERITAGE
OF ARIZONA AND FOR ITS
Architectural/Historical SIGNIFICANCE

Santa Cruz County Courthouse

IN Santa Cruz COUNTY
WAS PLACED ON THE
NATIONAL REGISTER OF HISTORIC PLACES
ON December 7, 1977

Governor of Arizona

State Historic Preservation Officer

NATIONAL REGISTER OF HISTORIC PLACES

Memberships range from $250 lifetime to $20 annual individual. Lifetime members receive a beautiful framed membership certificate with a colored photograph of the Courthouse. For more information, Friends' officers may be called: George Post at 281-8640; Helen Littlefield, 281-1925; Elvia Ahumada, 287-7522; or Robert and Naomi Lenon, 394-2951.

● Books by Alma Ready

- **Open Range and Hidden Silver** by Alto Press (1973)
  - "The book has very substantial merit and I congratulate you on a professional piece of work." — Norman Cousins, American political journalist, author, professor, and world peace advocate.

    The story begins in Mexico three centuries ago when it was known as New Spain. In a series of setbacks that would have destroyed a less resilient people, it includes the tale of Nogales, the town that started as a lonely peddler's shack on the railroad right-of-way and became the county seat, with its twin in Mexico just across the street.

- **Calabasas** by Alto Press (1976)

  - Calabasas Road doesn't lead to Calabasas any more but the town was real enough once.

- **Nogales, Arizona 1880-1980 Centennial Anniversary** by the Nogales Centennial Committee (1980)

  - This is a bibliographic gem, especially for those who are originally from Nogales, Arizona or Sonora, Mexico.

- **A Very Small Place** by Alto Press (1989)

  - "RAVE REVIEW" (from Random Jottings, by Brendan FitzSimons, *Nogales International*, Feb. 7, 1990): "Alma Ready's latest literary effort has drawn lavish praise from "Books of the Southwest," compiled monthly by W. David Laird of the University of Arizona. Laird writes: "Pardon a bibliographer's penchant for his own field, but it would be difficult to over-praise this small book. Ready has identified a goodly list of published sources of probable interest to anyone who wants to know more about Nogales and environs. (She) divided them into 11 categories to make browsing fun, described them bibliographically, and added annotations about contents, point of view, value, special characteristics, and such…it's an attractive publication. You'll like it."

◉ Magazine & Newspaper Articles

- "Charleston – THE TOWN THAT NEVER GREW OLD." *Arizona Highways,* Nov., 1962: (p. 2)

- "Charleston is Almost Gone." *Brewery Gulch Gazette* (Bisbee, Arizona), 25 April 1963: (page 1 ff.)

- "down where the GRASSES grow." *Arizona Highways,* June, 1963: (p. 30)

- "Manzanita." *Arizona Highways*, Oct., 1963: (p. 4)

- "Under-water Homestead." *Brewery Gulch Gazette* (Bisbee, Arizona), 09 Dec. 1965: (page 1 ff.)

- "The Armed Fugitive." *Arizona Days and Ways Magazine,* 18 Sept. 1966: (p. 17)

- "A Depot but no Train." *Arizona Republic,* 29 Jan. 1967: (p. 26)

- Photos. *Arizona Highways,* March, 1967: (p. 32 & 36)

- "Desert Winter Bouquet." *Arizona Highways,* Nov., 1967: (p. 28)

- "Impressions of Santa Cruz County." *Arizona Highways,* Feb., 1968: (p. 20)

- "Javelins Chase Couple." *Nogales International,* 30 Jan. 1970: (p. 1)

- "Calabasas: Return to the Old Southwest History." *The GAC Magazine,* Fall 1971: (pp. 17-21)

- "Ghosts Walk in the Huachucas." *Brewery Gulch Gazette* (Bisbee, Arizona), 3 April 1972: (p. 1)

- "Hard-rock drilling contest highlights: Nogales 1908 July 4th celebration." *Nogales International,* 4 July 1976: (p. 5)

- "Trees Dying" (photo) *Nogales International,* 10 Sept. 1977: (p. ?)

- "Once upon a Christmastime in the Santa Cruz Valley" *Easy Living,* Dec. 1977: (p. 8)

- "Foreign travel just out your back door." *Easy Living,* Jan. 1978: (p.4)

- Book review: "Saving the Queen." *Easy Living,* Jan. 1978: (p. 17)

- "Missions and mines are historical highlights in Sonora's Cananea." *Easy Living,* March 1978: (p. 8)

- "Sea turtle steak (at the Marlin)" *Easy Living* ("The Appetizer Restaurant Roundup)", March 1978: (p. 15)

- "Waiting for the tide at Kino Bay." *Easy Living,* June/July 1978: (p. 8)

- Book review: "Mawson's Will, the Greatest Survival Story Ever Written." *Easy Living,* June/July 1978: (p. 18)

- "GRINGO RANCHER: William Barnett of La Arizona, Sonora," by Alma Ready and Alberto Suarez Barnett. *The Journal of Arizona History. (Vol. 27, No. 2, (Summer, 1986), Published by: Arizona Historical Society):* (pp. 195-210)

◉ Photo-journalism Features:

Seen in Santa Cruz County – through the camera's eye

- "For Alma Ready – long-time hobby becomes career." *Nogales International,* 01 Feb. 1974: (p. 3)

- "For Milford Noon – Weather reports family tradition." *Nogales International,* 02 March 1974: (p. 3)

- "Venerable buildings." *Nogales International,* 17 April 1974: (p. 6)

- "When GOD gives us spring," *Nogales International,* 15 May 1974: (p. 6)

- "Trees." *Nogales International*, 19 June 1974: (p. 9)

- "But is it art?" *Nogales International*, 17 July 1974: (p. 9)

- "Flood Plains Management Plan." *Nogales International*, 7 August 1974: (p. 6)

- "Santa Cruz County Fair." *Nogales International*, 5 Sept. 1974: (p. 6)

- "October is the month…" *Nogales International*, 17 Oct. 1974: (p. 9)

- "Roads to Nowhere in Particular" *Nogales International*, 21 Nov. 1974: (p. 7)

- "It CAN Happen Here." *Nogales International*, 24 Dec. 1974: (p. 10)

- "Calabasas long silent." *Nogales International*, 6 Feb. 1975: (p. 8)

- "Firewood back in style?" *Nogales International*, 13 March 1975: (p. 8)

- "Southern Arizona's Spring Visitors." *Nogales International*, 24 April 1975: (p. 6)

- "Water in a Thirsty Land." *Nogales International*, 12 June 1975: (p. 8)

- "Summer Festival – Part 1." *Nogales International*, 17 July 1975: (p. 6)

- "Summer Festival [hunting toads]." *Nogales International* 7, August 1975: (p. 5)

- "School Days." *Nogales International*, 9 Oct. 1975: (p. 8)

- "Signs & Symbols." *Nogales International*, 27 Nov. 1975: (p. 9)

- "Spring Comes to Santa Cruz." *Nogales International*, 10 April 1976: (p. 7)

- "Montezuma Hotel – remnant from the past." *Nogales International*, 24 April 1976: (p. 5)

- "Quarter Horse Show Sonoita Style." *Nogales International*, 29 May 1976: (p. 7)

- "The unique mesquite" *Nogales International*, 24 July 1976: (p. 5)

- "Windmills." *Nogales International*, 4 August 1976: (p. 7)

- "They had to Make do." *Nogales International*, 18 August 1976: (p. 8)

- "September." *Nogales International*, 25 Sept. 1976: (p. 5)

- "Winter Wonderland in Southern Arizona." *Nogales International*, 29 Dec. 1976: (p. 7)

- "Depot." *Nogales International*, 9 March 1977: (p. 5)

- "Doors." *Nogales International*, 22 May 1977: (p. 2)

● Photo Contest Winners

Mamiya C-3 camera
(Mamiya-Sekor 80mm lens)

Prizes won in Photography

- Kodak Amateur Snapshot Contest, *Arizona Daily Star*, Tucson, Arizona

- Consistent winner in all categories 1953 through 1966 except 1964

- Several local Grand Prizes (city-wide)

- 1958 – $25 in National Finals, Washington, D.C.

- 4 June 1961 ("sheep shearers") – Merchandise, 1st prize, Class B, b/w adult & teenager activities.

- 10 June 1962 ("party noise-maker") – 1st prize, Class A, b/w babies & children.

- 24 June 1962 ("truck stuck in sand") – Honors, Class B, b/w adult & teenager activities.

"Serenity in Nature." Best in Class C Snapshot Contest — scenes and still life. Arizona Star: July 1957.

"Now where is the postman with our DESERT Magazine?" 2nd Prize. Desert Magazine: Nov. 1964 (p. 43).

"Sheep," somewhere on the Navajo Reservation (July, 1959).

Top Class C Entry
This nicely-framed photo of Window Rock on the Navajo Reservation gained a first class in class C (scenes and tabletops) for Mrs. Alma Ready, 1153 Rocky Way, in the sixth week of the Arizona Daily Star's photo contest (5 July, 1959).

- 1 July 1962 ("lizards") – 1st prize, Class D, b/w animals & pets.

- 1966 Honorable Mention in National Finals

Sylvania Electric Products, Inc, New York, N. Y. and Ford Motor Co., Detroit, Michigan
- 1959 $50. radio (Nationwide)

General Electric Flash Picture Contest, Cleveland, Ohio
- 1959 $10. in Bi-monthly contest (Nationwide)

The Stockman (mag) Phoenix, Arizona
- 1960 2nd Prize in Statewide Contest

Montgomery Ward, Tucson, Arizona
- 1961 First in Annual Southern Arizona contest
- 1961 Fourth in Annual Southern Arizona contest

Pima County Fair, Tucson, Arizona
- 1961, 1963 2nd Prizes in Annual County-wide contests.

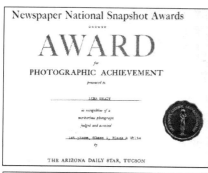

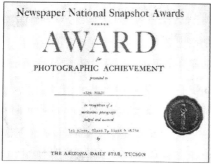

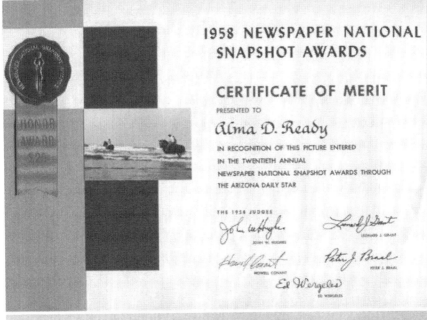

"Unusual Surf Shot in Winners' Circle." July 27, 1958. Best photo in Arizona Daily

About the Editor

Patrick Simpson is the second of Alma Ready's four sons. He was born and raised in Sidney, New York and later won two scholarships to Hartwick College in Oneonta, New York, where he majored in English. He was with IBM's Field Engineering group for nearly thirty years, retiring in 1991 as an Advisory Information Developer. Pat also freelanced as editor of the Raleigh

North Gideons newsletter and as occasional travel writer for Raleigh's Fifty Plus magazine. He once taught a travel writing workshop at the North Carolina Writers Network Conference in 2000.

In 1994, following Pat's earlier retirement from IBM, he and his wife Anne traveled literally around the world for a year, even though she was nearly wheelchair-bound by crippling Charcot joint disease in her ankles. After the doctor gave his OK she was determined to go. Pat wrote two books about their epic journey: *Wheelchair Around the World* (1998) and *Wheelchair Down Under* (1999). They later followed his ancestors' 1878 wagon-train trek across the U.S.A., which resulted in his third book, *Whither thou Goest* (2001), which won the 2004 JADA Press Nonfiction Book of the Year award. *Desert Angels*, his first historical novel (2011), is based on the Bannock Indian War of 1878.

Along the way, they met some of the most unforgettable people of their lives—all over the world and while visiting libraries, museums, Indian reservations and battle sites throughout the American West. They followed Indian warpaths and pioneer trails, including the entire Oregon Trail—twice! Their paths led them to such diverse places as the Nevada Governor's mansion, the U.S. Capitol Building, and a ghost-town cemetery in Hardman, Oregon.

Anne died in 2006 as a bilateral amputee with only one useable arm, as a result of complications from Charcot Joint Disease and necrotizing fasciitis, more commonly known as "flesh-eating bacteria." But she had proven over and over that one good arm and one good brain, with God's help, was enough to conquer nearly every problem. Her courage, strength, and strong faith inspired everyone who ever knew her or had heard of her.

Pat was blessed later on when he met and married Betsy. They live in

Pat & Anne Simpson at a book-signing for "Wheelchair Around the World" in Tampa, Florida, 1998.

Raleigh, North Carolina, home of the NC State Wolfpack and the Carolina Hurricanes.

In 2009 Pat began another journey as "Mr. Pat" when he felt called to be a volunteer at the Frankie Lemmon School, whose mission is to help preschool and kindergarten children with special needs to achieve their full potential. For over four years, until age caught up with him, Pat tried to give his "friends" one-on-one support by assisting the teachers once a week in any way he could. He also writes monthly updates for the Raleigh Rescue Mission's Boosters club and weekly updates for his Sunday school class.

***

(See Patrick Simpson's website at: **www.booksbypatricksimpson.com**.)

 At: Patrick Simpson

THE END

Happy trails, Mom.

Made in the USA
San Bernardino, CA
03 September 2015